THE MANSFIELD BREW

The present Board of Directors with a portrait of Claude Chadburn. Jock Nangle, (left), Philip Baker, Robin Chadburn and Tony Scruby, the Managing Director.

The Company Secretary with five Directors of Subsidiary Companies; Michael Parsons, (Head Brewer), Hector Chalmers, now deceased (Hotels), Hugh Wilson, (Properties), David Tyne, (Accounts), Fred Gleadell, (Secretary) and Richard Umbers, (Sales). Jack Williamson (Managed Houses) appears on page 146.

Philip Bristow

THE MANSFIELD BREW

At the invitation of the present Directors of the Mansfield Brewery, Philip Bristow has attempted to capture something of the history of the Company since 1850 and to relate its growth to that of this part of the East Midlands.

Despite every effort to ensure that information given is accurate and up-to-date, the Mansfield Brewery Company regret that they cannot accept responsibility for errors and omissions.

NAVIGATOR PUBLISHING LIMITED

RINGWOOD HANTS

First published in Great Britain by
Navigator Publishing Ltd, Ringwood, Hants

ISBN 0 902830 03 1

BY THE SAME AUTHOR

French Menus Interpreted
What Food Does What
Through the French Canals
Through the Belgian Canals
Down the Spanish Coast
French Mediterranean Harbours
Through the Dutch Canals
Round the Italian Coast
Through the German Waterways

Photoset, printed and bound
in Great Britain by
REDWOOD BURN LIMITED
Trowbridge & Esher

CLAUDE W. CHADBURN

7th February, 1888 – 27th February, 1977

Since this short history was printed
Claude Chadburn has died peacefully
at Papplewick Hall
We are publishing with happy memories
of a life dedicated to the Brewery.

Introduction

One hundred and twenty-five years may not seem a very long time to some enterprises, but we tend to forget what fundamental changes the country has seen come and go during that time, and this busy industrial area still shows the slowly healing scars created by the railways and early mining slag heaps. Coal mining and Mansfield beer are both looking optimistically to the future, and it has been a fascinating exercise putting together this account of some of the factors that have made up the Brewery's story.

What we have not achieved is enough of the humour and often downright comedy of some of the situations passed down with increasing embellishment by word of mouth – sometimes verging on the scurrilous by the time it has got to me!

We depend for our jobs here on the money that the early Partners risked in the business, and that their successors have continued to entrust to us. But brewing is the business of everybody here. We could not brew without the shiftmen, the foremen or the supervisors, nor could they operate without the backing of those of us who have to deal with paperwork. It is no good pouring wort or delivering beer into unsterile vessels, or not getting paid for doing our various jobs. So please forgive us if we seem to have concentrated on those who set the enterprise up rather than on the many who made it a success and who now have the responsibility for Mansfield Brewery's future. Here's to them!

ROBIN W. CHADBURN
Chairman

1

One hundred and twenty years is not a long time in the history of breweries and many were established in England before the commencement of the Mansfield Brewery in 1855. Some have endured in their original form, many have not; so many local brews have succumbed to that destroyer of character, the take-over and, to a lesser extent the merger, although Nottinghamshire is probably unique as a county in having so many breweries who have retained their independence.

The Mansfield Brew, once established and cared for with new techniques and improved production, has remained through the years with whatever integrity, special charm or flavour it was that made its name in the beginning.

In the original Partnership Deed of 1855 between William Baily, Samuel Hage and John Watson, a clause was inserted to the effect that the Partners 'shall be true and just to each other'; maybe a common enough legal term but the sentiment inherent in this phrase somehow permeates the Mansfield brew and brewery today, as though implanted in 1855 at Littleworth – where the brewery still is – this yeast of sentimental purpose has germinated over the years so that your deal with Mansfield Brewery is as 'true and just' today as it was in 1855. Your pint of Mansfield brew is much superior.

One tends to think of the 1850s as being peaceful and quiet, a general time of forelock-tugging peasantry; and to imagine that present-day man is unique in his problems, and that they are contrivances of the progress of the twentieth century. Yet one hundred and twenty years ago in June when John Watson left his brewing business at Sheffield and Samuel Hage his farm at Ollerton to come to Mansfield to sign with William Baily (following the coldest winter in living memory), the steam and machines of the Industrial Revolution had already secured complete domination. The spinning mule had been invented over seventy-five years earlier, blast furnaces using coal to make iron had been erected nearly a hundred and fifty years before; and Stephenson's engine had been hauling trains for twenty-five years. The Industrial Revolution was certainly still on the move.

The steam engine was busily dealing a death blow to the stage-coach trade which had enjoyed increased popularity between 1823 and 1849 and in the Mansfield area particularly.

The Partners are sure to have used Simpson's Robin Hood Coach which ran daily between Mansfield and Nottingham, leaving the 'Eclipse' in Mansfield Market Place at 8 a.m. and setting off on the return journey from the 'Black's Head Inn', Nottingham, at 4.30 p.m. And there were many others they could have used starting from stage-coach inns in which their brewery was later to have an interest. From Stirrup's Coach Office in Swan Inn Yard there was the Royal Mail Coach for London at 4 a.m.; the Hope for London at 1 p.m. and the Express at 5 p.m., the Champion for Manchester at 9 a.m.; the Volunteer for Liverpool at 8.30 a.m.; the Royal Hope to Derby at 1 p.m.; the Royal Union to York, via Worksop and Doncaster at 8 a.m.

Comfort apart, with their average speeds of about eight miles an hour it was obvious that the coaches could not compete with the railways. The Royal Union Coach, for instance, from York to Nottingham via Mansfield, was said to have a reputation for making good time but it still took eleven hours for the journey.

The 'Swan Inn' at Mansfield had probably been the foremost coaching inn with relays of post horses always in readiness in its large stables.

Only four years before the commencement of Mansfield Brewery the opening by Queen Victoria of The Great Exhibition in 'the palace made of windows' had been hailed throughout the country as a symbol of peace and prosperity.

Industrial Britain was jangling and restless with the effort of achieving the Industrial Revolution, of becoming the workshop of the world. To complement the exhaustion of his splendid industrial efforts the working man had been awarded a half-holiday each week by kind permission of the recent Factory Act. And as though dancing to the industrial jangle, the new leisure with more money was creating a demand for more amusement, any amusement. Nourished by new standards of social life the population grew rapidly (it was to grow from below ten million at the beginning of the century to over thirty million at the end). Much drink was consumed.

And in spite of the abysmal lack of understanding about cleanliness and its effect on health generally, it does seem to have been appreciated that alcohol acted in some measure as a sterilising agent.

It was a good time to start a brewery. Although many breweries had started in the previous century and the numbers of them had rapidly grown, the need to secure selling outlets had not seemed to occur to them. In the time after the Mansfield Brewery came into being brewers everywhere were realising the need to secure outlets for their beer and the tied-house slowly emerged; the brewer acquiring a new interest in public house property.

Previous owners, often brewing for their own needs in and around the back yard, had been hard pressed to up-date the premises, and began to find it impossible to keep up with the demands for proper drainage and reasonable comfort, coming on top of the local Health Inspector's demands. Breweries had been set up to satisfy the Customs & Excise demands, and had often lent money to publicans to allow them to keep pace with one set of demands, only to find that new rules made fresh demands, and the bricks and mortar were insufficient security for further loans. Thus a lot of indifferent properties found their way by default as a liability for brewers.

The business of Mansfield Brewery was founded during the Crimean War; not that far distant events had such an impact then as now when today's world appears nightly in every front room. The newspapers of Baily, Hage and Watson would have waited for news brought by the electric cable, news of the Crimean War which ended as the brewery was getting under way and, within a year, of the British Army in action again, this time in India. The electric telegraph would have brought news of the relief of Cawnpore, Delhi and Lucknow. The business of communications itself was stirring public interest, awe and speculation. Telegraph engineers were public figures and money that might recently have been speculated on railways now went on submarine cables and overland telegraphs. The Partners' newspapers would not have achieved the remarkable topicality that we take for granted today but the Partners would have been able to keep in touch with the trends of the licensed trade through the *Morning Advertiser*, first published in 1794 (and today Britain's second-oldest national daily).

The first Partners of Mansfield Brewery were brought up in an England that was still a traditional oligarchy – although they would have seen, and been part of, classes emerging through the wealth of trade to challenge the order based on hereditary privilege and to establish democratic government as a reality. The leadership of the country was in the complacent hands of Palmerston and the Whig nobility but the prosperity that was growing and spreading everywhere was inspiring in many the desire to be a self-made man. The emergence of the manufacturing interests in opposition to the landed interests had its beginnings in the Midland area of the Mansfield brew.

It was a time when the initial mania for railway building was abating somewhat. There were then about 2,200 miles of track in the country built in the twenty-two years since railways 'started' – or since the Stockton and Darlington Railway obtained its first Act; and over 3,000 additional miles of track had been authorised by Parliament on the application of over a hundred separate railway companies existing then.

The railway with the greatest impact on the Mansfield Brewery trade was the Midland, founded at Eastwood by colliery owners in 1832. These Nottinghamshire and Derbyshire colliery owners had previously enjoyed a monopoly of trade by sending their coal by canal to Leicester but the Leicestershire coalfields completed a railway from their mines to Leicester and took the trade away. The Nottinghamshire–Derbyshire coal owners responded with a railway – the Midland – from their mines to Leicester and thus resumed the battle for the profitable coal trade.

It is interesting to note that when Mr. Gladstone tackled the railway problem in his Act of 1844 he dealt with the possible terms of purchase by the State.

1845 is regarded as the peak year of the Railway Mania just as the 1790s are regarded as the time of the Canal Mania, from which it will be seen that the canals enjoyed at least fifty years of prosperity and coal carrying.

Baily, Hage and Watson were probably influenced to set up their brewery by the industrial developments that were taking place around them and had taken place in the preceding years. It would certainly be true to say that the Nottinghamshire coalfield was revolutionised between 1840 and 1849 by the coming of the railways, and coal miners were known to be amongst the thirstiest of beer drinkers. Apart from the connections to the coal mines, railway building did not develop very rapidly in the area when compared with other parts of the country; but having been instrumental in developing the coal mines they had served their purpose for Mansfield Brewery.

Mansfield Brewery had ready made thirsts of long standing for coal has been mined in Nottinghamshire since the 13th century. In the 16th century there was big development in the area below Mansfield and to the west of Nottingham and evidence of the wealth of coal began to appear. Wollaton Hall was built by Sir Francis Willoughby around 1585 and it was estimated that half the output of the Nottinghamshire mines was produced at Wollaton alone. Coal was mined in the Byron estates in the Newstead–Papplewick area, of passing interest to this history since the president of Mansfield Brewery, Mr. Claude Chadburn, has made his home at Papplewick Hall since 1926, and it stands on an isolated column of unmined coal.

From the 17th century coal mining developed at a steady rate of progress and iron smelting furnaces too, but transport was the problem for the roads were simply rutted tracks of mud. As a result canals were built, the first in the Nottinghamshire area being the Cromford Canal, connecting to the Erewash Canal, and to the River Trent. When the Cromford Canal was built the intention was to extend it to Mansfield but the contours of the ground presented too many problems, it was proposed in 1788 as an extension of the Erewash Canal upwards to Pinxton and was intended to serve the iron furnaces at Butterley and Somercotes, limestone quarries at Crich, lead works at Alderwasley, Cromford where Sir Richard Arkwright's cotton mills were and towns such as Matlock, Belper, Wirksworth, Alfreton and Mansfield, but the arrival of the Birmingham and Derby Junction, the Midland Counties and the North Midland Railways took away practically all the canal traffic except that on the Grantham and the Trent.

The Cromford Canal ran from a junction with the Erewash at Langley Mill, up the valley to what is now Ironville where the Pinxton branch left it. The main line then swung west, passed through the Butterley Tunnel, 2,966 yards long, to Bullbridge where it crossed the Amber on an aqueduct and at Ambergate turned up the Derwent valley to Cromford, crossing the river one and a quarter miles from Cromford by an aqueduct thirty feet high.

Chesterfield however, a good deal farther from the Trent than Mansfield, overcame contour problems; the Chesterfield Canal, forty-six miles long, from Chesterfield fell by five locks to Staveley, rose by fourteen locks to Norwood Tunnel which was 3,000 yards in length, and then fell by forty-six locks to the Trent. Thus there were obviously some contours to be overcome in the building of the Chesterfield Canal but perhaps they were more fortunate in their surveyor and designer than the proponents of the Mansfield venture. Chesterfield employed the great James Brindley in 1769 to make the survey for their canal which opened eight years later, on 4th June 1777. Nineteen years later the Trent was linked to the Thames, Mersey and Severn.

In 1800 a short branch canal was made from near the Derwent aqueduct to the wharves of Peter Nightingale at Lea Wood where there were lead works and cotton mills. It is interesting to note that the owner of these wharves was the father of Florence Nightingale who was establishing the first base hospital at about the time Mansfield Brewery was founded; she arrived in the Crimea before the Battle of Inkerman and in no time reduced the death rate to a twentieth of what it was. And of course the influence and example of this lady from Lea Wood extended far beyond the Crimea, probably to every hospital in the world and certainly in the setting up of the Red Cross in 1864.

In addition to the coal carried on the Cromford Canal there were big cargoes of stone to improve the roads and to build the railways. The canals carried the materials that destroyed them.

The collieries and quarries and ironstone works moved their weighty production down to the canal side on horse-drawn railways, the specially laid lines sometimes being over a mile long and known as tramways or tramroads. There were quite a number and one of particular interest was the Mansfield–Pinxton line. This route had been thought of as a canal in 1803 but it materialised as a tramway in 1819. The construction of it, under the patronage of the Duke of Portland, was initiated by the coal owners of the Erewash Valley but the people of Mansfield lent their enthusiasm to the project which, as with all railway promotion schemes, needed the approval of a special Act of Parliament. The Mansfield–Pinxton Railway carried the stone and lime which Mansfield produced, plus the Erewash Valley coal, to the Cromford Canal at Pinxton and then via the rivers

Trent and Soar to markets in the south.

The Railway Company with Gentlemen of the town partook of a most excellent dinner provided for them by Mr. Stirrup at the 'Swan Inn'. Great numbers of workmen were entertained at different public houses in the town, including the 'Waggon & Coals' later bought by the Brewery and featured in a very old photograph of the horses and wagons. It is interesting to note that this old hostelry was sold as recently as 1970 to make way for road improvements. The influence of transport requirements clearly continues to have its effect. They were celebrating the arrival from Pinxton Colliery of the first ten wagons, each loaded with two and a half tons of coal on top of which sat workmen and colliers bearing branches of laurel. Bullocks, and later horses, pulled the wagons; when descending gradients men walked beside the wagons 'spragging' the wheels. At that time Stephenson's locomotive had been running at Killingworth Colliery for five years.

The railway reduced the price of coal in Mansfield from 10s. to 8s. a ton. Apart from this benefit Mansfield needed to transport the stone for which it was becoming increasingly well known. It was also building up a big trade for good quality moulding sand.

Although Stephenson's 'Locomotion No. 1' engine had drawn goods and passengers over the Stockton and Darlington Railway as early as 1825, the first time that Mansfield saw an engine, known as 'Puffing Billie', was in August 1849 when a contractor's engine arrived. And a month later Midland directors arrived to open formally Mansfield station; in October the Mansfield–Nottingham line was in business. Most people have a vague idea where Nottingham is and even Sheffield, and in between them Chesterfield is often referred to as the very centre of England, but Mansfield is perhaps not so often visited. It is a real Midlands town, not north and not south. Not on a main route between larger centres, and in spite of all the rail activity at the time of the Brewery's foundation – not now having any passenger rail link at all. Mansfield is situated in the heart of the rich North Nottinghamshire coalfield. It is a market town standing on the River Maun from which it takes its name, although the river is so depleted now that it could barely justify description as a stream; indeed a bottle tossed into the water as it passed the brewery at Littleworth would often not find sufficient depth in which to float. (That has not stopped it causing havoc and devastation between the Brewery and the Tin Works in time of flood, with water pouring over the cills of ground floor windows at the 'Bridge Tavern' right up to 1975.)

The town seems always to have experienced a geographical exclusiveness, a splendid isolation. The canal building fever came near but never nearer than Pinxton; the early railways scattered lines everywhere but avoided Mansfield for many years, even during the railway building mania, in fact fifty years after the Railway Mania the ambitious scheme of the Lancashire, Derbyshire and East Coast Railway to run a line from Chesterfield to Lincoln (in fact it ended at Pyewipe Junction) did not include a diversion to Mansfield.

The long-established coalfields lay along the Nottinghamshire–Derbyshire border and when they were extended it was to the east, the railways eagerly flinging out connecting lines. The population of Mansfield has grown mainly through the development of the mines.

There are old cave dwellings at Rock Hill and an ancient British settlement is supposed to have preceded a Roman encampment there. Spearheads of brass and stone have been found locally, made before the Romans introduced the use of iron. Many Roman coins and relics have been discovered, coins of Vespasian, Constantine and Marcus Aurelius. The Roman Fosse Way, from Exeter to Lincoln, ran through Nottinghamshire some twenty miles from Mansfield; in fact the central position of the county has contributed largely to its history.

Because of its central situation in Sherwood Forest Mansfield was a hunting seat of Mercian and Norman kings; was in the possession of the Earls of Chester and passed through the Hastings and others to the Dukes of Newcastle and from them to the Duke of Portland. The forest was well known as a hunting ground and in the time of Edward the Confessor, William the Conqueror and William Rufus it was a Royal demesne.

'The Miller of Mansfield' will be familiar to all acquainted with the exploits of Robin Hood in Sherwood Forest. The forest once covered the whole eastern side of Nottinghamshire; even now it occupies an area about twenty miles long by about seven miles wide on average and, of course, the coal mines have encroached. A lot of Sherwood Forest was heathland and scrub in the late 18th century. In the early 17th century only about ten per cent was forest and there had been a great deal of destruction between the Maun and the Meden by the disastrous fire of 1624. During the Civil War every tree was felled from Clipstone Park and during both World Wars trees were felled.

To the north that part of the forest in The Dukeries has been preserved; the great parks of Welbeck, formerly belonging to the Duke of Portland; Clumber, now National Trust and at one time the property of the Duke of Newcastle; Worksop, at one time in the ownership of the Duke of Norfolk and Thoresby that belonged to the Duke of Kingston.

The Mansfield Brewery trade blends industry with romance. They are fortunate to have on their doorsteps the working thirsts of many miners (working the most successful mines in the country), and the leisure attractions of The Dukeries, Sherwood Forest and Robin Hood. Romance and industry certainly exist side by side. Edwinstowe, for instance, is spoken of as the gateway to the old Sherwood Forest. Here, at St. Mary's Church, it is said that Robin Hood married Maid Marian. And here at Edwinstowe today you will find the headquarters of the North Nottinghamshire Area of the National Coal Board. Not that coal intrudes quite so obviously as you would expect from the number of mines in the area. The contours of the countryside are there as camouflage, headgear is somehow often hidden away and tips are wrapped in a blanket of green. What one cannot hide is the tell-tale darkened hedgerow, the five-o-clock shadow of trees and bushes.

As you would expect, the names of the hotels, pubs and inns of the Mansfield Brewery reflect the area they serve: 'The Dukeries Hotel' atEdwinstowe, the 'Portland Arms' in Mansfield, 'The Miners' Arms' at Alfreton plus other 'Miners' Arms' at Brimington, Grassmoor, Ashover, New Whittington and Pinxton. The Merry Men of Sherwood Forest are represented by the 'Little John Inn' at Ravenshead and by a selection of 'Robin Hoods' at Bakewell, Blackwell, Edwinstowe and Rainworth. You will also find a selection of seven Mansfield Brewery pubs around Sutton-in-Ashfield, near which are the Robin Hood Hills.

In Mansfield Brewery country naturally you believe in Robin Hood despite the fact that historians are not agreed as to his origin. After a pint or so of Mansfield Brew, you are happy to accept that Robin was an actual victim of the ruthless forest rule of the Norman kings. His exploits are found in Scott's *Ivanhoe*, Tennyson's *The Foresters*, Alfred Noye's *Sherwood* and Ben Jonson's *Sad Shepherd*. If he was man and not myth he was probably seven hundred years too early to have sampled the delectable Mansfield brew.

The forest was a very real hazard for travellers round Mansfield. The rutted road through Thieves Wood, within a mile of the town, slowed down travel on the hill to less than walking pace and made easy victims of wagon teams going to and from Nottingham, and the business of carrying the mail often required a good deal of nerve.

But Mansfield can boast of some famous sons: John Roberts, the first worker of double-point net lace in frames; James Murray, inventor of the circular saw, Joseph Tootel, inventor of fluted or grooved rollers used in cotton spinning, now known as stretchers. The Dolphin lamp posts on the Embankment were made at a Mansfield foundry and, later, George V letterboxes. The family of Lawrence Sterne (*Tristram Shandy, Sentimental Journey*), lived here.

There was a mustard mill in Mansfield from which grew the firm of Barringer, Wallis and Manners who found that the metal boxes containing their mustard possessed greater trading potential than the mustard itself; and thus they concerned themselves with the manufacture of metal boxes which led on to their joining the giant Metal Box Company. The present Chairman of Mansfield Brewery is married to the granddaughter of I. H. Wallis, one of the founders of Barringer, Wallis and Manners, all family names well known in Mansfield and rightly respected for their service to the town. Isaac Henry Wallis was Mayor and lived at Crowhill House when Crowhill Drive was a private road, and members of the families appear continually in old records and on old photographs recording the town's historical progress.

And for a royal connection, apart from the hunting interests in Sherwood, Mansfield can claim to have almost made a king. James, First King of the Scots, was proclaimed King of England on 31st March 1603 at the Market Cross in Mansfield by the Sheriff of Nottingham.

Fifty years later George Fox, the founder of the Society of Friends, held many ministrations in Mansfield and Mansfield Woodhouse. He converted many over a period of five or six years before being jailed at Nottingham, and there is still a strong Quaker element in the community – certainly the Barringers and the Wallises and the Manners were all 'Friends'. Probably very anti-Brewery, and one hopes the present family alliance with the Chadburns has not disturbed too much their rest, in spite of the re-siting of the Quaker burial ground due to road works recently.

When a little disturbance has seemed appropriate the worthy citizens of Mansfield have proved that they are not lacking in spirit, as witness the Opposition to the Militia Act in 1757, the Bread Riot in 1800, the Luddite Riots in 1812, the Reform Bill Riot in 1831 and the Chartists Riot in 1839.

2

When the Mansfield Brewery started, Mansfield was the centre of a rising agricultural district and following the enclosures of the previous century much of the surrounding land was held by the big landowners: the Portlands, Devonshires, Rutlands. Elsewhere in England agriculture was suffering from absentee landlords, high rents and short leases.

But into the extensive farming interests of the area the coal mining industry spread as a result of the large undeveloped coalfield lying close to Mansfield; and such a splendid source of energy naturally attracted other industries: cotton and other mills, iron foundries. A quarter of the population was engaged in the hosiery industry. The stone quarries had contributed to Mansfield's importance by supplying stone for the part rebuilding of the Houses of Parliament, St. Pancras Station and many other important buildings at home and abroad.

When the business of brewing in Mansfield was first established in 1855 by the formation of the Partnership, land was acquired in small plots from various owners at the lower end of Littleworth adjacent to the River Maun. And there was water available from bore-holes through the natural sand-stone.

The land purchased then was more than was needed for the buildings then required, but the surplus was used for land for the dray horses, and pigs were reared on the spent grains. Later a good deal of land was sold to build a railway, but now that has been re-purchased and expansion has used up every available inch.

Then, in 1855, the Partners agreed that 'the said business shall be carried on under the firm of The Mansfield Brewery Company in the premises now occupied by the said Partners in Littleworth in Mansfield aforesaid.'

With the farming interests of Baily and Hage it is likely that the Partnership was formed with the aspects of agriculture in mind in addition to brewing, for Mansfield was a malting centre of considerable importance. In 1843, for instance, it is recorded that nearly 15,000 qrs of malt were made in Mansfield. In those days Mansfield malt was as famous as Mansfield moulding sand was to be later. Up to the 1850s there were twenty-six malt houses active in the town. Most were small, one-man houses, often adjoining a public house and drawing their barley supplies from the surrounding farmlands. The barley was conveyed in sixteen-stone sacks even up to the Second World War, a tribute to the strength of the men who handled them. By modern standards the barleys used then were of poor quality but they were used locally until after the turn of the 19th century, and through the First World War.

Most of the buildings used as malt houses have disappeared or have been joined on to other buildings (as in Eclipse Yard and Grove Street). The largest of these old floor maltings in Midworth Street was used until a few years ago, when the difficulties of manning it became insuperable and its construction unsuitable, on a site often threatened by road planners.

Before the railway era malt was carried by pack mule or heavy wagon to places as far away (in those days), as Derby and Sheffield. By 1920 the only malt houses operating in Mansfield were the two owned by the Brewery, in Midworth Street and Grove Street (the latter was damaged by fire about 1930, closed and sold).

Hop-growing in the Nottinghamshire area was big business at one time since *White's Directory* of 1832 lists sixty growers but it did not last long when it was realised how poor the quality was, and by the time the Mansfield Brewery started hop-growing had ceased commercially in the area. Hops belong to the nettle family and it appears that they are not easy to grow in the British Isles although, for many years, Kent has emerged as the most favoured county with Herefordshire; Worcestershire also producing hops of good quality. The soil and climate have to be exactly right for the cultivation of hops and even then they have to be looked after like invalids from Spring to September. Quite large quantities are imported from America, the Dominions, and Europe.

Flemish immigrants first grew hops in Kent at the beginning of the 16th century and, of course, beer as such was not known in this country until beer-with-hops was introduced from the Continent; until then the English drink was ale.

The outline of the old Brew House and Fermenting Room can be seen in the modern photograph below. In the group are Gordon Jervis, (Fitter), Albert Gregory, (Painter), Ian Boucher, (Electrician), John Ruskin and Brian Rose, (Fitters).

In brewing, the matured female flower of the plant, the hop cone, is used as it contains the essential oils and resins.

The Partners would have dealt with raw materials that have not changed over the years although some methods of production have changed, particularly with increased knowledge of bacteriological functions, sterilisation and refrigeration; and scientific knowledge has enabled a better quality of basic materials to be obtained. But basic principles and materials remain just as they were centuries ago. Malt is now bought in bulk from areas of the country where the best barley is grown – Lincolnshire, Suffolk and Norfolk. Hops are bought from Kent, Herefordshire, Sussex and Worcestershire as well as from Europe.

Sugar is imported from the West Indies, refined in London and transported in bulk liquid form by road tanker. In referring to the sugar used in beer making it is interesting to note that one of the suppliers to the Mansfield Brewery, the firm of Manbré and Garton, started business in England in 1855 also. In the history of Manbré and Garton it is recorded that Alexander Manbré came to England from Valenciennes in the year that Mansfield Brewery was founded; and that he introduced glucose sugar to lighten and sweeten the heavy beers of that time. Before then, according to this history, the heavy-tasting liquor, powerfully malted and hop-laden, had long discomfited the beer drinking community by causing drunkenness to a stage we never experience today; also that in the same year William Garton, a Hampshire man, had started the production of Sacharum, or invert sugar, using the patent of his brother Charles. This patent was described an 'an improved method of treating cane sugar, to render it fitter to be employed in brewing, wine-making and distilling'. It was the beginning of what Manbré and Garton claim to be the 'complete revolution' in brewing. This may well be so with certain beers but the whole business of brewing is concerned with the fermentation of sugars which are primarily derived from the malt by conversion of the starch; the sugar so derived, for instance, is sufficient for the making of some stout, with no addition.

Although it might be imagined that satisfying the thirsts of the miners was the first consideration when Baily, Hage and Watson started, it was to be another thirty-five years before the large collieries in the Mansfield area were getting under way and attracting labour in considerable numbers. Other industries were growing as well: iron foundries, mills and the stocking industry deriving power from water mills.

The factors that influence the setting up of most industries are concerned with availability of material and labour, with the business of production; and if the resulting product makes a popular splash the sales outlets then spread out as limitless as ripples in the ocean. The setting up of a brewery was different in that the demand for their products was localised and they grew where there was a need for them, in a way the demand existed before the brewery, the thirst before the beer.

There is very little reference in old records to any sort of public-house brewing in Mansfield and it was certainly not on a scale that existed in other parts of the country. Towards the end of the 17th century public-house brewing had declined in favour of specialist brewers who began to emerge in the middle of the 16th century. Derby and Preston were two of the last towns where pubs brewed their own beer and there were also a number of survivors in the Black Country.

John Watson will have been aware of the thirsty potential, indeed he may have wondered if he could spare sufficient time from his Sheffield brewery for the new Mansfield venture. In the Partnership Agreement he provided that 'he shall be at liberty if he thinks fit at any time during the continuance of the said partnership to substitute his son, John Watson, upon the same terms.'

William Baily was the initiator, the driving force behind the new brewery enterprise. His occupation is shown in the Agreement as Gentleman and it is not known if he had any experience of the brewing industry. Samuel Hage was a farmer at Ollerton and it may well be that he was a supplier of barley to the malthouses of Mansfield. The expert knowledge and experience needed to establish the enterprise came from the third Partner, John Watson, brewer of Sheffield.

Their new enterprise was to cater for an increasing population. The first half of the 19th century had been notable in this respect, mainly because of improved medicine and not on account of an increase in the birth rate. In the twenty years between 1841 and 1861 the population of England, Scotland and Wales rose from 17 million to 23 millions.

The demand for coal was rising continuously. The Pinxton Coal Company was formed in 1847, for instance, and not only did Mansfield's proximity to such new sources of labour guarantee a large supply of hot, thirsty miners but plenty of coal was available for steam raising and power supply. During the second half of the 19th century there was a considerable increase in the numbers of miners required, in fact the demand for more and more labour continued until after the First World War. In the fifty years prior to the war the number of miners nationally doubled but in the Mansfield area, from the time of the founding of the Brewery up to the First World War the number of coal miners in the area increased four-fold. The attraction was not in the nature of the job, needless to say, but in the wages paid. In this agricultural community a miner could earn two and a half times as much as a farm labourer and for shorter hours worked.

Although coal has been mined in the Nottinghamshire area since the Middle Ages the real development of coal mining was coming about at the time that the Mansfield Brewery was formed. District Mines Inspectors were first appointed in 1850, for instance, when faulty ventilation, amongst other matters, was causing concern. And in 1856 steam came to lend a hand to weary limbs.

Among the men who found much-needed comfort in the Mansfield brew there were many who had started in the pits at the age of seven, an age considered mature enough then to be in charge of ponies below ground. Can one wonder at a man having a life-time thirst when his childhood has been spent down a mine in a seam less than three feet high, dragging away baskets of coal for hour after hour, to be exact from 6 a.m. until 8 p.m., working almost naked and encouraged far too often by kicks or blows? And what horror it must have been for any child even getting down to his place of employment since there were no cages then. Descending the shaft into the mine meant clinging to the chain that hauled up the coal although the younger children were held in the arms of a miner who sat in a loop of the chain. But imagine men and children clinging like flies to a chain that was free to swing from side to side as it lowered them into the black pit.

At the time Mansfield Brewery was started in 1855 there were no children of six or seven working in the pits; the Mines Act of 1842 had forbidden the employment of children at such an age. Six-year-olds who had been denied employment by the Mines Act were just about eligible by age to enter a public house when Mansfield Brewery started.

The Mines Act of 1842 was a reflection of public concern in legally forbidding the employment underground of children under the age of TEN. Fortunately for the mine owners it was about the time that haulage machine power was beginning to appear and it replaced the labour of the younger children. Although machine power would have cost more than the nine-pence to a shilling a day paid to the children for their fourteen-hour shift, the machine produced more profit and fewer tears.

At one time a daily allowance of beer had been part of a miner's wages and, despite the Truck Act of 1831, there was still a fairly widespread custom of paying part of a man's wages in kind, particularly from the taverns and ale houses. During the first five years of the Mansfield Brewery they may have inadvertently received some of this custom.

It is not suggested that the miner needed much inducement to exchange his hard-won wages for beer. The traditional mining village has always concentrated its leisure hours around the public house and later the institute or club; and miners have always been well experienced in the beer drinking league. Who can wonder at it?

One competitor for the miner's leisure in the early and middle part of the 19th century was the Methodist Church. Like many reforming bodies they were influenced by the exceptional to reform the average. Undoubtedly there was drunkenness and brutality then just as there is today. But the Methodist influence did not end by seeking to separate a man from his pint. The chapels gave men some hope at a time when hope was sorely needed in their lives; inspired them, taught them, equipped them to seek improvement in their conditions when conditions were crying out for improvement. To their credit some of the more enlightened colliery owners encouraged the chapels.

Men who went on to fulfil talents away from the pit face owed the beginnings of their scholarship to the Methodist Church. Naturally the reforming zeal only touched the fringe of the minority; had it been otherwise this history might never have been written. A hundred years before, in fact, the great Methodist Revival had been a real challenge to the public houses.

The opportunities for learning and improvement obviously appealed to those anxious to seek knowledge but also attracted men with natural qualities of leadership, men anxious to lead the attack for better working conditions. Trade Unions were slow to organise in the Nottinghamshire coalfield. There was a strike of sorts in 1844 which resulted in the defeat of the miners and it was not until nearly twenty years after that a Miners' Union appeared, only to struggle and fail. Men who struck were locked out of their jobs and ejected from company houses. Strike leaders were not only victimised at their place of employment but were stopped from obtaining any employment in any other mine, the employers forming themselves into associations against the unions. But despite the efforts of the coal owners to discourage the formation of unions and despite their employment of professional strike breakers whenever trouble for them threatened, the strikes focussed attention on the problems of the miners and some benefits were achieved, such as a limitation in the numbers of hours worked; the evils of the Truck system were also exposed.

In addition to the encouragement offered by the Methodist Church there were other opportunities opening up for the working man. The Mechanics Institutes date from the era of Baily, Hage and Watson although the Mansfield Institute was early upon the scene, opening in 1831. These institutes provided leisure and recreational facilities for the working man. It is interesting to note that the present Mansfield Town Football Club had its origins in the Mansfield Mechanics Institute.

Football and cricket were popular in most mining communities. Many collieries formed their own brass bands and competed against each other at enthusiastic rallies. Gardening was another useful diversion for the miners and most coal owners provided good gardens to the colliery houses which helped to occupy the men in the summer when the coal trade was insufficient to provide full employment. From the gardens developed the well-attended Flower Shows at which the miners displayed their produce, pigeons and cage birds. Such shows were the high spots of otherwise drab lives as were the Wakes Weeks, a time of rejoicing for the participants and for the Brewery. For the children the Annual Sunday School treat was an event of sufficiently breathless excitement to guarantee attendance on fifty-two Sundays of the year.

The accepted holidays were Christmas Day, Good Friday and Whit Monday.

3

In less than a year, and before the Mansfield Brewery Company had properly got under way, there was a Dissolution of Partnership. On 24th April John Watson, the Sheffield brewer, relinquished his interest in the Mansfield Brewery, the remaining Partners paying him £450 for his share.

The Crimean War had just ended with the signing of the Peace of Paris on 30th March. In Paris also, in this year, Louis Pasteur began the studies that were to lead to a later revolution in the production of all beers including the Mansfield brew.

It is easy to be critical of John Watson for getting out at the beginning of what was to become a successful enterprise. At that time Sheffield had far greater possibilities than Mansfield. For probably five hundred years Sheffield had been building up a reputation in the iron trade and for a hundred years or so before John Watson's time it had specialised in the cutlery trade. Now the iron and steel industries were struggling to meet the demands of the railway era, and of the American market for steel.

If civic recognition may be taken as a barometer of the commercial importance of a town it may be observed that Sheffield was incorporated as a borough in 1843, an honour for which Mansfield was to wait almost another fifty years.

After Watson's departure, William Baily and Samuel Hage continued to devote their time to the business of brewing for the next seven years without any noticeable change in the affairs of the Brewery at Littleworth or in the town of Mansfield. In the big world outside the Indian Mutiny had come and gone as had the American Civil War and the Anglo-Chinese War. The National Miners' Association had been founded and the Mines Regulation Act introduced, the first English tramway had been drawn by horses through Birkenhead, the typewriter had been invented, the Queen's beloved Albert had died, Chancellor of the Exchequer W. E. Gladstone had reduced income tax to sevenpence, then to fourpence, Charles Darwin had published *The Origin of Species* and John Stuart Mill *On Liberty*.

The trade of the Mansfield Brewery had developed to the stage where the partners considered that they might keep the profits of malting within the family. On 12th November 1863 they set up in business partnership as Maltsters 'under the firm of Hage and Baily' and with a capital of £6,000, divided as to £3,000 in the name of Samuel Hage, £1,500 in the name of William Baily and £1,500 in the name of William Hage. In this agreement Samuel Hage and William Baily described themselves as Wholesale Brewers of Mansfield. William Hage was shown as a Farmer of Bilsthorpe.

The population was growing, trade was growing and, with it, the demand for coal; the prosperity of the mines being stimulated by the development of railways to serve them. But although the mineral traffic increased, the Mansfield area was still not regarded as passenger trade potential by the new railway tycoons. Although trade tended to build up where railways served, at the outset railways tended to go where the trade was.

After the opening of the branch line to Mansfield in October 1849 the station remained a railway cul-de-sac without much prospect of any new developments of lines in other directions. The Midland Company were looking outwards to extend their boundaries.

In 1864 the Great Northern Railway were also seeking to extend their boundaries and looking towards the promise of the Nottinghamshire coalfields, also to the Dukeries that was not served by railway.

Of this threat the Midland Company were aware and also of the lack of communications between north and south Nottinghamshire including the termination of the railway at Mansfield. In fact, in 1860 they had submitted to Parliament a Bill for the building of a line to Worksop but the Dukes of Newcastle and Portland were at cross purposes regarding the route to be taken over their land; it took them until 1864 to agree.

The Midland Company then had to fight off proposed invasions of their territory by the Manchester, Sheffield and Lincolnshire Railway and the Great Northern but the necessary Bill was passed and they commenced work on the Mansfield–Worksop line. From the cuttings at Langwith the stone was used to construct the bridge north of Mansfield sta-

The 'Old Brown Cow' on Ratcliffe Gate, Mansfield was rebuilt at the time of the coming of the railways but the stone bridge that adjoined has now disappeared. The Pub is built into the local sandstone from which the old Rock Houses, higher up, were fashioned.

tion; the fifteen spans, reaching a height of about sixty feet, carried the line over Church Street. It continued on over Bath Lane, over Woodhouse Road into Mansfield Woodhouse, through Pleasley Junction, Shirebrook, Langwith, Elmton and Cresswell, Whitwell, past the Steetley quarries and so to Shireoaks South Junction, joining the line of the N.S.&L. Railway with one branch to Worksop and the other towards Sheffield. This new line from Mansfield was opened in 1875, the same year that 2nd Class fares were abolished by the Midland Company.

The Royal Commission on Coal had revealed that about fifty million tons of workable coal lay beneath the area served by the Midland branches extending from the Mansfield area.

Some authorities refer to the Coal Fever of 1872–3, others to the Coal Famine of 1871–3; perhaps the one produced the other. In the period 1871–3; due to scarcity, coal prices rose to over £1 a ton; a few years later the price was less than half this figure. We complain today about price fluctuations and shortages as though they are a new phenomenon: indeed we have been a long time learning. In the time that we have developed wireless, motor-cars, atomic energy, men on the moon and television we have failed to understand how to regulate supply and demand.

Five years after William Baily, Samuel Hage and William Hage set up as Maltsters another malting partnership was formed that was to have some influence on the history of the Mansfield Brewery.

The firm of Shacklock and Titley, Maltsters, was set up on 4th November 1868 and this was of particular interest because Henry Stephen Shacklock was the cashier of the Mansfield Brewery Company. The other partner in the business of maltsters, Addison Titley, was to feature in the history of the brewery for many years. At the time of the establishment of this partnership he is shown as a Gentleman of Mansfield.

Addison Titley was a well-connected young man of twenty. His grandfather, whose second wife was Mary Addison, had established a successful flax spinning business in Leeds. He was the chairman of the Liverpool, London and Globe Insurance Company, a director of the Midland Railway and a Justice of the Peace.

The flax spinning business was carried on by Addison Titley's father who married Mary Hage of Bilsthorpe; thus the link was established with Baily and Hage, the Maltsters, and Baily and Hage of the Mansfield Brewery.

Addison Titley's father was a good-natured eccentric with a passion for orchids, horses and travel. Often the family would set off for an afternoon drive that would extend to one of the Channel ports and then to a sea crossing and then to a considerable tour of the Continent . . . dressed and equipped for an afternoon drive. In the days before passports or travel formalities such impetuous excursions were possible of course.

No member of the family had any connection with malting or brewing before young Addison Titley joined in partnership with Shacklock. They subscribed in equal shares to the capital of £1,600.

Looking back it is interesting to note that Addison Titley's connection with malting and brewing covered the period of the alternating Premierships of Gladstone and Disraeli, a period of stable and continuing progress, of much-needed reforms leading to a considerable increase in middle class influence.

In 1871 the Sale of Commissions were abolished in the Army, one of many reforms brought in by Gladstone's Secretary of State, Edward Cardwell. Another proposal that did not succeed was a Licensing Bill put up by the Temperance Section of the Liberal Party. From that time the brewers and the drink trade interests flew into the welcoming arms of the Conservative Party.

In 1871 the Mansfield–Southwell railway line opened. Southwell was already connected with the Nottingham–Newark–Lincoln line by a single line from Rolleston Junction opened in 1846. Coming up from Southwell the railway passed through a steep cutting at Python Hill where the family home of the founder of the Mansfield Brewery was situated; in fact the bridge across the cutting was named Baily's Bridge.

The line came on and in to Mansfield, crossing Southwell Road by a girder bridge 66ft long; past the old racecourse and on to an embankment, over a girder bridge by the brewery at Littleworth, over the L.N.E.R. Mansfield–Nottingham line, over the viaducts built of Mansfield stone and in to Mansfield station.

Through Shacklock, Addison Titley became interested in the affairs of Mansfield Brewery and was employed by Baily and Hage either in the brewery or in their malting business, at the same time running the small malting business that he shared with Shacklock. Trade was improving. On 15th November 1873 Addison Titley was admitted to the Partnership of the brewery.

'Whereas William Baily and Samuel Hage have been The Mansfield Brewery Company,' read the new agreement, 'they agree to admit Addison Titley into Partnership in consideration of £2,000 for a sixth of the ascertained goodwill.'

The brewery premises, however, remained in the ownership of William Baily and Samuel Hage to whom Mansfield Brewery paid a rent of £377 per annum. For insurance purposes the brewery premises were then valued at £4,130.

Seventeen years earlier when John Watson had left the Partnership his third share of total assets was valued at £450. Now, on Addison Titley joining, his sixth share was valued at £2,000 excluding any interest in the premises.

The shares in the brewery in 1873 were apportioned as to five-twelfth each to William Baily and Samuel Hage and two-twelfths to Addison Titley. Profits were, of course, taken in those proportions but labour was not.

The agreement stipulated that 'Addison Titley should devote the whole of his time to the said business and diligently employ himself therein and promote to the utmost of his power the benefit and advantage of the partnership and shall receive for his services £150 per annum.'

Whereas 'neither of the said William Baily and Samuel Hage shall be obliged to attend to the said business any further than they shall think proper and may either actively engage in the said business or abstain wholly or partially from any active part therein . . . and the said Samuel Hage may continue to superintend and manage so long as he shall think fit to do so and shall have the sanction in that behalf of the other partners and while continuing such superintendence shall be paid £250 per annum.'

By arranging to receive brewery profits in return for wholly abstaining from the slightest effort to produce them Baily set a precedent that was to serve his family handsomely for over a hundred years.

At this stage of development the brewery needed a young man in command. The original Partners had been running it for nearly twenty years and were getting tired. Addison Titley was then twenty-five years of age, keen to succeed on his own and possessed of an impeccable financial background.

He must have been impressed with the prospects of Mansfield Brewery to pay £2,000 for such an opportunity but events were to prove that his judgement was sound enough in this respect. At the time the Agreement seemed loaded against him but it gave him a foot in the door that was to open half way for him in less than five years time, in other words to give him a half share of Mansfield Brewery.

The 1873 Agreement just mentioned – the agreement that admitted him – in addition to allocating him a two-twelfths share, made further provision that on the death of William Baily or Samuel Hage he, Addison Titley, was to have the option of purchasing one-fifth of their shares, subject to William Baily nominating his son, William Edward, and Samuel Hage nominating his son-in-law, Fothergill Watson; in that event the nominees were to give their whole time and attention in like manner with respect to the said Addison Titley. The Baily heir, William Edward, emerges later in our history, two months later in fact for William Baily died on 5th January 1874. Of Fothergill no more is heard. William Baily left all his real and personal estate to his only son, William Edward.

The late William Baily, joint founder of the Mansfield Brewery Company, was one of five children. His younger sister, Sarah, had married Francis Chadburn by special licence at Blidworth in 1846. Francis Chadburn, who was then 29, had been farming at Wicker Leys, Southwell. He died at the age of 47 at Cockcliffe Hall and Sarah went to live at the Baily home at Python Hill, surviving Francis by 41 years. They had a son, William Jackson Chadburn, who was destined to feature largely in the affairs of the Brewery. This destiny was by no means apparent to the young William Jackson Chadburn, however, when he was engaged in business as a Maltster in Mansfield.

It has already been noted that Henry Stephen Shacklock, the cashier of Mansfield Brewery, set up in partnership as a Maltster with Addison Titley in 1868 in the style of Shacklock and Titley, Maltsters; and that five years later Addison Titley succeeded to a partnership of the Brewery, an opportunity apparently denied at that time to Shacklock. In 1877 Shacklock set up in partnership as a maltster again, this time with William Jackson Chadburn. Like Addison Titley before him this association with Shacklock was to lead W. J. Chadburn on to a Partnership in the Mansfield Brewery although not for another eight years. During that time the malting affairs and the brewing affairs were no doubt conducted in a friendly and intimate relationship and indeed a family relationship so far as William Jackson Chadburn was concerned, since he had assisted his Uncle Baily as a brewer's clerk from the beginning of January 1875.

The business of Shacklock and Chadburn was started on 5th October 1877 with a capital of £2,100, of which Shacklock subscribed £1,400 and Chadburn £700. The business was carried on at the malting house and premises in the Eclipse Inn Yard, West Gate, in Back Lane West and in Ratcliffe Gate, all in Mansfield.

Understandably Shacklock took two-thirds of the profits and Chadburn one-third. The books of Shacklock and Chadburn, Maltsters, were kept at Mansfield Brewery. When, from time to time, it was necessary to obtain sureties for Malt Duties these were entered into by John Baily of Python Hill, elder brother of William Baily, joint founder of the Brewery, and William Jackson Chadburn's uncle.

By his association as a maltster with Shacklock in 1877 William Jackson Chadburn set foot in the wings of the stage he was to dominate, for the greatest development and progress up to that time at Mansfield Brewery took place during his command. The surprising thing is that, in view of his relationship to the Bailys, he did not join the Brewery in 1878 when two of his cousins formed a new Partnership with Addison Titley.

This new Partnership was established in 1878. The last Partnership Agreement had seen Addison Titley alloted a minor proportion of the shareholding and a maximum allotment of the work and it was remarked that he must have been impressed with the prospects. Now, less than five years since the date of that agreement, William Baily and Samuel Hage were dead and Addison Titley was in a position to call the tune. The new Partnership Agreement, dated 1st March 1878, was between Addison Titley, William Edward Baily and his uncle, John Baily.

Addison Titley took a share of six twelfths, William Edward Baily four twelfths and John Baily two twelfths. It was determined that only Addison Titley should have the superintendence, at a salary of £600 per annum; the other two were to take no active part in the business.

This agreement was signed in March 1878 and the profit for that year was £1,200. In the following year the superintendence of Mr. Addison Titley blossomed for the profit increased five-fold to £6,000 (in 1879). And in the three ensuing years Mr. Addison Titley did very well to return profits of £4,800, £8,400 and £6,000.

The public houses leased and purchased at about this time were:

LEASED	*Rent* £
'Anvil Inn', Mansfield Woodhouse	14
'Bowl in Hand'	50
'Crown and Anchor', Exchange Walk, Market Place	50
'Royal Oak', Stockwellgate	70
'Red Lion', Blidworth	40
'Kings Head'	49
'New Inn'	45
'Brown Cow'	35
'Star Inn', Commercial St.	35
'Lord Byron'	40
'Carpenters Arms', Newgate Lane	40
'Woolpack', Sutton	70
'Forest Tavern', Skegby	14
'William IV'	50
'Traveller's Rest', Sutton	35
'Old White Bear Inn'	55
'Duke of Wellington', Kirkby	32

PUBLIC HOUSES AT COST PRICE

Year bought		*Price* £
before 1877	'Railway Inn', 'Ram Inn', 'Wheatsheaf', 'Portland', Sutton	6,133
1877	'King's Arms'	1,700
1877	'Black Horse', Stockwellgate	1,650
1877	'King and Miller' and cottages, Chesterfield	2,150
1878	'White Bear', (Site of Victoria)	2,140

1878	'Cross Keys', Westgate	3,500
1879	'Pheasant' and 3 cottages	1,100
1879	'Reindeer' and 15 acres	2,100
1880	'White Swan', Mansfield Woodhouse	555
1880	'Elm Tree', Scarcliffe	820
1880	'Blue Bell', Sutton and 2 cottages	1,370
1880	'Mapplewells' and 7 acres	825
1880	'Parliament Oak', Mansfield Woodhouse	800
1881	'Royal Oak', Ollerton	485
1881	'Hope and Anchor', Mansfield	800
1881	'Industry', Shirebrook	1,250
	19 Houses	TOTAL: £27,378

A valuation of the company's assets was carried out in 1877 for the Balance Sheet of 1882:

	£
Brewery land and cottages	7,072
Horses, carts, harness, pigs	1,000
24 Fermenting vessels, Engine Boiler, Mash Inn, Coppers, Piping etc.,	2,000
Stock of beer and malt	1,400
Stock of beer and hops	3,500
6,000 casks at 12s. 6d.	3,750
New stables	600
Cash	655
Public Houses	27,378
	£47,355

The area was progressing. The Stanton Company had sunk the first mine to the west of Mansfield at Pleasley. There was progress in the mines too, for they were going over to fan ventilation. The Midland Railway wanted to build a new locomotive shed for twelve engines at Mansfield which would make the town quite a railway centre. The Great Northern Railway had opened an Erewash Valley Line and were about to open a Leen Valley Line. There was fierce competition between the railway companies and although, later, there were Coal Traffic Agreements to protect railway rates, the competition between the railway companies was greatly appreciated by the colliery owners.

The profit of 1879 was achieved despite a serious slump in the country and the record profit of 1881 was achieved following a winter of unprecedented severity. It was the famous year when the Thames froze over, when there was a sheep roasting on the ice near Eel Pie Island, when 20,000 were estimated to be skating on the Serpentine.

Nearer to home the ice-boats were unable to force a passage for the barges on the Central Midlands Canal. Snow drifts everywhere were so formidable that snow ploughs with eight horses were unable to get through.

The record Brewery profit of 1881 was also a reflection of profitability elsewhere. In that year the Nottingham lace factories were so busy that their machines were running practically day and night and the collieries were fully employed to meet the demand for steam coal.

The railways were still expanding. Branch lines were built between the Erewash Valley Extension and the Mansfield–Nottingham line. These developed passenger traffic considerably, for instance the first branch from the Mansfield Line at Radford to the Erewash Line at Trowell made through running possible between London and the North via Nottingham; the first London–Bradford Express passed over it on the 1st June 1880.

In 1881 the Nottinghamshire Miners' Federation came into being, with branches at Arnold (a lot of the Bestwood miners lived there), Annesley, Clifton, Wollaton, Whitemoor, Bestwood, Newstead and Cinderhill, all in or near the Leen Valley. There had been already in existence a South Yorkshire Federation and an association in Derbyshire. In fact, elsewhere Trade Unionism had become accepted and in the year that W. E. Gladstone was elected Prime Minister it was apparent that the Liberals were conscious of the power of the Trade Union vote.

After the failure of their strike in 1844 and their brief re-emergence in 1863, the Nottinghamshire miners were at last on the point of organising themselves into a position of strength. Although, of course, strikes were organised then for the same reasons as now; and over the years how many pints of the Mansfield brew have been downed in support of vociferous arguments in support of more money or less hours or both. Until now strikes had been settled on the owners' terms because the unions had lacked the resources to resist.

Religious interests may have been somewhat piqued at the prosperity of the Brewery; they will certainly have wondered if this prosperity was being obtained at their expense. A census was carried out one Sunday evening in January 1882, the object being to establish if church attendances were being seriously affected by Sunday evening attendances in public houses.

There were no licensing hours then, of course, so that hardened drinkers could have attended church without cutting into a limited number of drinking hours available.

However, the census was taken of the number of people at evening service in the fifteen churches of different denominations in Mansfield and of the number of people in the fifty-seven public houses. Out of a total population then of about 13,500 there were 2,703 people in the churches and 750 in the public houses; but it should be mentioned that the count was taken between 6 p.m. and 8 p.m. and although it must have given some satisfaction to the religious census-takers who initiated the count, the drinking fraternity will have realised that concentrated pub attendance is inclined to take place later in the evening.

Christmas was, and still is, the busiest drinking time and then there were other convivial drinking occasions such as the fairs that were always well attended. At the Martinmas Hiring Fair the men would line up on one side of 'High Street and Station Street' carrying the emblem of their particular skill, farmers would pass up and down looking at them and give the shilling that was binding.

There was also the Nottingham Goose Fair, and three or four Mansfield fairs. Vast quantities of the Mansfield brew would be drunk and there would be ample displays of tempting food, gooseberry pork pie and rook pie.

4

Addison Titley lived at Gilcroft House at the top of Brunts Street, a large house in large grounds; so large, in fact, that they would enclose what is now the area all round from St. Peters and round Blind Lane, and Church Side.

He was sheltered by inheritance from the absolute necessity of earning his living but he needed an interest and the affairs of the Brewery linked in well with his maltings in Midworth Street. Although he owed his Brewery opportunities to Baily and Hage he might well have considered that he had repaid with the profits he had earned for them, for William Baily Senior in particular.

When Baily's place as principal recipient of profits was taken over by his son, William Edward Baily, the ever courteous Addison Titley decided to set a time limit to his generosity. It may also have been that Titley, a modest and retiring little man of great charm, found it difficult to appreciate the extrovert antics of Edward Baily; perhaps he did not find them so attractive as the eccentricities of his father.

Edward Baily had a retinue of lay-abouts whom he dressed in some sort of uniform, earning them the title in Mansfield of Baily's Horse. Within the portals of Baily's fine house in West Gate there permanently lurked a member of Baily's Horse, waiting to force upon any unsuspecting visitor a pint of Mansfield Ale.

Baily's sole interest in the Brewery lay in the amount of money he could extract from it, although he was also to appreciate the value of the space it afforded to assemble and accumulate his collection of stuffed birds. It must have come as a welcome relief to the Brewery employees when this collection was taken to a separate building to form the nucleus of the Mansfield Museum where, for many years, the Baily Collection could be viewed. The space in the Brewery yard was required for more fermenting vessels.

Edward Baily had married the daughter of the landlord of the 'White Hart', Mansfield and about the time that their daughter was born, in 1884, he was spending a lot of time in Penzance, for his health it was said.

However, after twelve years, Addison Titley had had enough of running the Brewery single-handed and, at the age of thirty-six, was discussing the question of his retirement with the company lawyer, William Bryan. A half share of the brewery was owned by Addison Titley and the Baily interest owned the other half.

It was agreed that Addison Titley should dispose of his share and the new Partners of Mansfield Brewery emerged in 1885 as William Edward Baily, Henry Stephen Shacklock – previously noted as the cashier of the Brewery who had entered into a Partnership with Addison Titley in 1868 as Maltsters and again with William Jackson Chadburn in 1877 – James Handley Hopewell of the Lounge, Albert Street, Mansfield described as a Wine and Spirit Merchant and last, but by no means least, William Jackson Chadburn.

In this new Partnership W. E. Baily inherited from his father the proposition that in return for receiving the greatest share he should do nothing whilst Shacklock, Hopewell and Chadburn were required diligently to employ themselves to the utmost of their power. Baily's share was three sixths and the others one sixth each, W. J. Chadburn securing his share through a mortgage arrangement with Addison Titley. The salaries were to be £300 per annum to Shacklock and £200 each to Hopewell and Chadburn.

Since it was agreed that Hopewell might give a fair proportion of his time to the wine and spirit business that he had established, and since Shacklock had been employed at the Brewery for around twenty years it was clear that the fresh enterprise needed was going to come from the third and most junior of the three working partners. At the age of 35 and with a newly arrived baby (his eldest son Francis), it was an opportunity that William Jackson Chadburn needed as much as the Mansfield Brewery needed him. Many breweries had fallen by the wayside and many more were to do so.

Although Addison Titley had disposed of his financial interest in the Mansfield Brewery he continued to supply them with malt from his large malt house just across the way in Midworth

Street. He had married Matilda, a daughter of Dr. Thomas Godfrey of Mansfield, and they had five sons. When he decided to take a rest from his labours at the brewery he was 37 years of age. His eldest son, Edward, was ten and the family decided to celebrate their father's release from the daily grind by taking a long holiday in Scotland.

Travelling fathers beget travelling sons it seems, and Addison Titley certainly inherited his father's desire to see the world; not that the purposeful Matilda would have permitted the impromptu excursions that her husband had enjoyed as a child. But throughout their life Addison and Matilda Titley travelled constantly, mainly in Italy, France, Switzerland and Norway. As an excellent shot and skilful fisherman Addison Titley frequently indulged his pastimes throughout England and Scotland in addition.

When at Gilcroft House, however, he visited the Brewery almost daily and appreciated the new atmosphere of business efficiency and the charm of W. J. Chadburn just as Chadburn appreciated his experience of running the Brewery. They got on well and it was a pity that they were never to be Partners together. In 1891 Mrs. W. J. Chadburn became a God-parent to Guy, the fifth and youngest son of Addison and Matilda Titley.

Baily was well out of the way for most of the time as he was developing his own line of interests in Penzance. Baily's Horse were still in commission but were not a source of embarrassment in the absence of their commanding officer.

William Jackson Chadburn was fortunate to have the opportunity of building up the Brewery business although it is likely that a man of his strength of purpose and character would have made his mark in any career, with or without a ready-made opportunity. He was a steadfast man, a keep-at-it-man, he knew he was the one with the vision. In any gathering he would stand out as The Gaffer.

The new Partnership came into effect on 1st January 1885 and in April they bought 'The Old Eclipse' in West Gate, Mansfield for £3,350. In July they bought 'The Bowl in Hand' in Leeming Street for £2,000.

In the following year, despite a serious slump in the country, they bought the 'Speed the Plough Inn' at Sutton-in-Ashfield for £1,250, the 'Peacock Inn' at Hucknall-under-Huthwaite for £1,375, the 'Forest Tavern' at Annesley Woodhouse for £1,020.

In 1887 they bought the 'Dial Hotel' in the Market Place,

Mansfield for £3,000, the 'Stag and Pheasant Inn' in Leeming Street for £2,200, the 'Railway Inn' at Pinxton Station for £2,000, the 'Queen's Head Inn' in Queen Street, Mansfield for £2,400, the 'Ram Inn' at Mansfield Woodhouse for £750, the 'Wagon and Coals', Ratcliffe Gate, Mansfield for £1,680, the 'Forest Tavern' at Skegby for £870.

In 1888 the 'Angel Inn' at Clowne for £1,675, the 'New Inn' at Mansfield Woodhouse for £1,380, the 'King's Head Inn' at Stockwell Gate, Mansfield for £1,600.

In 1889 the 'Plough Inn' at Ollerton for £800, the 'Old White Bear' in Station Street, Mansfield for £1,610, the 'Rifle Volunteer' at Skegby for £1,161, the 'Queen's Head Inn' at Alfreton for £1,100, the 'Yew Tree Inn', Woodhouse Road, Mansfield for £970, the 'Old Trooper Inn' at Sutton-in-Ashfield for £2,100.

William Jackson Chadburn was in his element. He now had two sons, Francis Ludlow and Claude William, and a daughter, Dilly. The Brewery provided him with the scope he needed to provide for his growing family. And as an up-and-coming business man he found time to interest himself in the affairs of the town; he loved involving himself in any special celebrations that were being organised. The Queen's Jubilee, for instance, was celebrated in a number of ways on 20th June 1887. To commence, a well-attended soirée was held in a marquee in the Market Place where the special attractions were Ethiopian minstrels and great American grotesques plus magical entertainment. A dance followed in the Town Hall.

Next day the town presented a gay and festive appearance with flags, banners and bunting decorating many buildings plus five triumphal arches of evergreens. Thanksgiving services were held after which there was a procession led by the Mansfield Brass and Reed Band and followed by the Improvement Commissioners, the clergy, Committee Members, the Sherwood Rangers Yeomanry Cavalry led by Lieutenant Starkey, the 4th Notts Rifle Volunteers led by Captain Foljambe, representatives of Lodges and Sick Societies, the Workhouse Drum and Fife Band, the Band of Hope Union and finally the fire engine drawn by four horses and with a postillion at the rear.

After the procession a dinner was given in the marquee for three hundred and eighty old men, then four thousand children were provided with capital teas at their respective schools as a reward for singing 'Rule Britannia' in the Market Square.

Finally a meat tea was laid on in the marquee for four hundred and seventy old women and the day's rejoicings terminated with a balloon ascent from the Recreation Ground.

Back at the brewery W. J. Chadburn was also arranging to lease public houses; anything to achieve more outlets. During his early years they arranged to lease the 'Carpenters Arms' at Mansfield for £40 a year, the 'Horse and Groom' at Mansfield, the 'Horse and Jockey Inn' at Leeming Street, Mansfield for £45 a year, the 'White Hart Inn' at Hucknall-under-Huthwaite, the 'Royal Oak Inn', Mansfield.

Once he had decided upon the acquisition of a property, completion was pressed forward with urgency by W.J.C. and the long-suffering solicitor Bryan was often in difficulty through the dilatoriness of the Commander of Baily's Horse. As a partner the signature of William Edward Baily was necessary on the acquisition of any property but he was not a man who replied to letters and certainly not to bills. He did not throw them into the waste-paper basket as some eccentrics do but filed everything meticulously, attaching the sixteenth application for payment of a bill – whether for six shillings or sixty pounds – to the carefully saved pile of fifteen previous applications.

When he had lived in West Gate the solicitor was able to call for Baily's signature with no greater inconvenience than the regulation pint of beer thrust upon him by the duty guard of Baily's Horse; but when Baily disappeared to Penzance the solicitor could only send off the documents for signature and follow them up with a series of telegrams. On one occasion when a deadline was imminent the solicitor succeeded in getting Baily as far as the St. Pancras Hotel, London for his signature.

Industry was humming all around Mansfield and W.J.C. was keen to take advantage of it. The last stage of development of the smaller branch line railways was completed and the coal trade was at its height with new mining villages springing up all around.

From 1889, for the next few years, the first large collieries in the Mansfield area were developed. They were the large pits of Kirkby Summit, Bentinck, Cresswell and Warsop and the smaller South Normanton Colliery.

The Bolsover Company followed the Stanton Company (who sank the first mine to the west of Mansfield, Pleasley in 1877), sinking mines to the north and east of Mansfield, Bol-

Gilcroft House in 1890, home of the Titley family until 1906. It was demolished for road widening in December 1970.

The opening of the Baily Museum in Mansfield.

sover Colliery opening in 1890–1.

In this year, 1891, another event was organised of a nature that was dear to W.J.C.'s heart, not only because he loved to be in the midst of busy municipal affairs but particularly when they also fitted in well with a boost for the trade of the Brewery.

Such an event was the granting of a Municipal Charter to Mansfield, the great event of 1891, the greatest event of the century in Mansfield.

Tuesday, 14th July 1891, was Charter Day at Mansfield, a day of public rejoicing when the Incorporation Committee returned from London bringing back the voluminous document bearing an enormous seal and the signature of Her Most Gracious Majesty Queen Victoria. The Charter of Incorporation secured to Mansfield the dignities and privileges attaching to a Municipality and William Jackson Chadburn was prominent in the organising of this great event.

The Brewery, shops, factories and schools were closed for the day. The town was decorated at considerable expense but a newspaper report gave assurance that the arrangements showed every good taste, in fact never before in its centuries of history had there been such an enthusiastic and unanimous exhibition, indeed the Town Hall reminded one of nothing so much as the scenes of illumination in Russia on state occasions. This splendid effect was achieved by illuminating the whole of the facade and upper windows with coloured lights from gas jets, with festoons of flags and bannerettes, shields, scrolls, the Royal Arms, Union Jack, crystal lights, much crimson and gold.

The Market Place was decorated with turkey red masts festooned with white and red paper roses from which Chinese lanterns were suspended at night. The 'Market Hotel' had a number of flags flying, the Brewery's newly acquired 'Dial Hotel' displayed five-foot crystals plus crowns bearing the letters V.R., laurel wreaths, shields and rustic devices. There were Prince of Wales feathers and blue and gold aprons at the 'Bull Hotel'; Mansfield Brewery's 'Old Eclipse' was prominent with crystal lights and a decorative V.R. shield surrounded by rose, shamrock and thistle. Fairy lamps outlined the 'Nag's Head Inn' which was also prominent with a display of flags and an illuminated star. At the 'Cross Keys', however, the decorative invitation 'Welcome to the Cross Keys' was rather frowned upon.

But in Stockwell Gate the 'Greyhound' displayed a sign, 'Drink health to our New Mayor, At the "Greyhound" not the "Hare".' The 'Black Horse' was somewhat enigmatic with, 'The Horse, find the Mayor.' The 'Horse and Groom' displayed flags and shields, the 'Red Lion' went in for evergreens over an illuminated crown.

Evergreens were also the choice of the 'Crown and Anchor' in Queen Street and of the offices nearby of the Inspector of Nuisances.

The 'White Hart' in Church Street went in for a crown and cushion in crystals. In Nottingham Road there was not much in the way of decoration, the 'Old White Bear' and 'Portland Arms' being content with evergreens; but Leeming Street was splendid with flowers and flags at the 'Masons Arms', flags and evergreens at the 'Stag and Pheasant', a sign inviting you to Drink Success to Our Charter at the 'Green Dragon'.

On the morning before the great day William Jackson Chadburn and other members of the Incorporation Committee proceeded by train (in a saloon carriage!), to London to receive the precious document at the Home Office. They returned the next day, reaching Mansfield at 1.12 p.m.; and as they steamed into the station a peal of Grandsire Trebles was rung from the Parish Church.

Outside the station carriages awaited them and they joined a procession through the town led by a Guard of Honour of the Mansfield Company of the 4th Notts Volunteer Battalion. There were thirty-five decorated vehicles in the procession representing the Mansfield industries, the contribution of Mansfield Brewery consisting of two conveyances decorated with hops, malt and a brewing vat.

For two hours or more the procession crawled around the town, through the cheering crowds that packed every street and vantage point, until the time for the principal event of the day was reached, the reading of the Charter in Market Square. From the spacious wooden platform, decorated additionally with the colourful dresses and bonnets of the lady ticket-holders, the Provisional Mayor, Mr. Hibbert, spoke; the Acting Town Clerk read the Charter; County Alderman Pickard proposed hearty congratulations and William Jackson Chadburn seconded the resolution.

The large gathering moved to the Town Hall then, and here Mr. Alton, of the 'Midland Hotel', had prepared a lunch of

Members of the Town Council, including W. J. Chadburn, (second from left behind the driver), setting out for the South of England to bring back the 'Pioneer' Steam Bus.

Mansfield's first and only steam bus. The sectional solid rubber tyres proved too difficult and unreliable.

roast beef, lamb, chickens, ham, pressed beef, pigeon pies, ducklings, tongue, lobster salad followed by tarts, jellies, trifles, fruits, creams, custards and pastries. The drink offered was Rüdesheimer, St. Julien and Perrier Jouët. There were speeches by the Provisional Mayor, the Deputy Provisional Mayor, Lieutenant Starkey of the Mansfield Troop of the Sherwood Rangers Yeomanry Cavalry, Mr. Elliott-Smith, Alderman Oates and then, as a slight diversion, Miss Ames sang 'In the chimney corner'.

Then the Provisional Mayor spoke and Mr. Savage spoke and the Provisional Mayor spoke. Mr. Sam Gilbert managed to get in 'Tom Bowling' and then Mr. White spoke and Mr. Sanders spoke and the Reverend Maples spoke and Mr. White spoke again.

On the Recreation Ground were roundabouts and acrobats and conjurors and hand-bell ringers and bands; there was dancing on the grass to an excellent quadrille band. At night there were illuminations and fireworks arranged by Mr. J. Pain of London. Over 8,000 people came to Mansfield by train alone and from places as far as thirty miles away.

And so the great day ended; although the revelry went on far into the night the police reported that the amount of drunkenness was less than that experienced on an ordinary Saturday night in Mansfield.

On the following day the less fortunate members of the community were remembered, the inmates of the Workhouse and the aged and poor. William Jackson Chadburn was one of the volunteer carvers at the dinner to seven hundred and fifty, the meal being laid out in a marquee in the field by the Cattle Market.

Over 30,000 people were present at the reading of the Charter. The roads and stables around were jammed with brakes and gigs. Such a sight had never before been witnessed in Mansfield and it was not expected that it would ever be witnessed again.

During the 1890s William Jackson Chadburn was also interested in a body known as the Mansfield Railway Commissioners; they were appointed to report on the town's railway services and achieved some improvement in facilities by the retiming of some Mansfield–Nottingham trains. What they were hoping for was another railway company to serve the town and provide better service and lower fares through competition.

They had approached the M.S.&L.R. and the G.N. with no success. The G.N. were of particular interest because they owned King's Cross and Euston.

The Commissioners turned to the L.D.&E.C. Railway who appeared willing to construct a branch line from their line near Warsop. A hitch occurred because the railway company wanted a level crossing in Pelham Street, in Mansfield, but the town had experienced the inconvenience of a level crossing when the Midland Railway had one at Portland Street.

The proposal fell through and later the Great Central bought the L.D.&E.C. Railway.

The Mansfield Railway Company came into being because there was a general desire for another railway to serve the town, the G.N. and the L.D.&E.C. Railway having failed to provide; also because the coal owners wanted a railway of their own to bring an end to the monopoly rates being charged by the Midland Railway.

The railway proposed was only ten and a half miles long, enough to connect with the Great Central Railway at either end, at the main line at Kirkby in the south and near Clipstone in the north. The Great Central Railway was naturally delighted to co-operate in having coal and other traffic delivered to them.

Despite his municipal activities W. J. Chadburn found the time to continue with his property buying campaign. In 1890 the Brewery bought a beer off licence in Portland Street, Mansfield for £800, a butcher's shop adjoining the 'Nag's Head Inn', Mansfield for £530.

In 1891 they bought the 'Old Spot Inn' at Pleasley Hill for £2,300, the 'Railway Inn' at Kirkby-in-Ashfield for £3,600, the 'Travellers Rest Inn' at Sutton-in-Ashfield for £1,300.

In 1892 the 'Robin Hood Inn' at Sutton-in-Ashfield for £2,600, the 'White Lion' in Church Street, Mansfield for £900, the 'Brown Cow Inn' in Ratcliffe Gate, Mansfield for £1,300, the 'Bird in Hand Inn' at Blidworth for £1,100, the 'Boot and Slipper Inn' at Swanwick for £1,025, the 'Bull Hotel', Mansfield for £1,620, the 'King William IV' at Stockwell Gate, Mansfield for £2,200, the 'Woolpack Inn' at Sutton-in-Ashfield for £3,300.

In 1892 the first telephone was installed in Mansfield and when the National Telephone Company issued its first directory in 1895 there were 22 subscribers in Mansfield. (The telephone service was not taken over by the G.P.O. until 1912.) W. J. Chadburn did not care for the instrument at all and was most reluctant to use it. When it rang he would instruct someone else to listen to it and say that whoever it was that wanted to talk to him should come to the Brewery to do so.

Continuing with the acquisition of new premises, in 1893 the 'Apollo Tavern' at Sutton-in-Ashfield was purchased for £2,250. This was the year of the Coal Mining Lock-out, the first big mining conflict that the men won. The year before Keir Hardie, then Independent Labour M.P. for West Ham South, had spoken at a National Miners' Association Rally at Eastwood.

The purchasing of properties went on with the 'Devonshire Arms' at Sutton-in-Ashfield for £3,250 in 1894, also the 'White Hart Inn' at Hucknall-under-Huthwaite for £1,900.

In 1895 the 'Little John Inn' at Edwinstowe for £700, the 'Portland Arms' in Albert Street, Mansfield for £3,725, the old 'Lord Byron Inn' at Mansfield for £1,240, the 'Old Eight Bells Inn' at Church Street, Mansfield for £2,860. The site of the 'Dukeries Hotel' at Edwinstowe was bought for £543.

In 1896 the 'Robin Hood Inn' at Rainworth was bought for £3,250, the 'Bridge Tavern' at Bridge Street, Mansfield for £2,800.

In 1897 the 'New Inn', Mansfield for £4,100.

In 1898 the 'White Lion' at Blidworth for £1,260, the 'Red Lion' at Blidworth for £800.

Apart from these purchases, others were still leased. W.J.C. had a way of learning when an inn or hotel was likely to become available and he would set the ever-patient solicitor Bryan to pursue the faintest opportunity. If his initial enquiry elucidated the possibility of another acquisition for the brewery, W.J.C. would set off immediately with Bryan in tow.

Before they successfully concluded the leasing of the 'Hop Pole Hotel' at Ollerton from Lord Savile, for instance, no fewer than fifteen meetings and excursions were organised by W.J.C. and Bryan.

It was Lord Savile who entertained King Edward VII at Rufford Abbey. In 1899, and again the following year, Edward, Prince of Wales, travelled on the Lancashire, Derbyshire and East Coast Railway between Tuxford and Ollerton. He usually arranged to pay a visit to Nottinghamshire in September each year and it so happened that his visits coincided with the St.

200–250 Barrels per week 1899
1902 Wine & spirit brought to brewery.
STABLES

REAR: Cellar Man; F. Brailsford; * ; F. Challand; *; J. Mellors; *; T. Place.
MIDDLE: J. Woodward; J. Woodward; J. Welton; R. Holmes; *; M. Cooke; J. Robinson; A. Watson; Willis Ward.

FRONT: W.J. Chadburn; *; B. Hind; T. Robinson; E. Smith; H. Seagrave; *; G. Shacklock.

Leger at Doncaster. In previous years he had come by road from the Great Northern station at Tuxford to the home of the Duke of Portland at Welbeck Abbey.

In 1903, when he was then king, he stayed with Lord Savile at Rufford Abbey. This was the first time that the Lancashire, Derbyshire and East Coast Railway had carried a reigning monarch on its line. Ollerton Station was completely repainted. The Royal Train, belonging to the Great North of Scotland Railway, arrived at Tuxford hauled by a gleaming G.N. Railway Atlantic Class locomotive; this was replaced by a resplendent L.D.&E.C. Railway 0–6–2T engine for the short run to Ollerton. But on race days the train was hauled between Ollerton and Doncaster by a dirty old G.N. Atlantic, according to a loyal subject and L.D.&E.C. Railway stalwart. In 1904 the G.N.S. train was used again but in 1905 the famed L.N.W.

* not named.

Railway Royal Train appeared. The following year Ollerton Station was decorated by gardeners from Rufford Abbey and the King arrived in the L.N.W. Railway Royal Train.

Railways interested W.J.C. as potential sales outlets and the Brewery became tenants of the Refreshment Room on Edwinstowe Station in 1897 although they were represented in better style at their newly opened 'Dukeries Hotel' nearby. The L.D.&E.C. Railway had first carried passengers from Lincoln to Edwinstowe on 15th December 1896.

Early in that year W.J.C. was busy with the proposals to build the 'Dukeries Hotel'. Apart from structural considerations it was necessary to secure agreement regarding the granting of a licence. It was proposed to remove the Full Licence from the 'Plough' at Ollerton and transfer it to the new 'Dukeries Hotel' at Edwinstowe and to remove the Beer On Licence from the 'Little John Inn' at Edwinstowe and transfer it to the 'Plough'. The 'Little John' licence was to lapse and it was necessary for W.J.C. tactfully to explain this to the tenant, as, also it was necessary for him to keep the tenant of the 'Plough' happy. In addition W.J.C. sought to enlist the cooperation – even to the extent of an appearance at Court – of the General Manager of the L.D.&E.C. Railway, also to prevail upon local landlords to support or, at least, not to oppose, the licence for the new 'Dukeries Hotel', and to sound out the views of Police Superintendent Brown in the matter.

Even when an informal provisional promise was received that the new 'Dukeries Hotel' would be licensed, if constructed in accordance with the plans submitted, there was still a great preparation of printed notices regarding the change-over of licences and these notices were posted widely, including such obvious places as the site of the 'Dukeries Hotel', the 'Plough', the 'Little John', the door of Edwinstowe Church and also at Ollerton Church.

The licence was granted by the Quarter Sessions at Retford on 21st October 1896. Very shortly afterwards the L.D.&E.C. Railway were complaining that all was not well at the Edwinstowe Station Refreshment Room so perhaps W.J.C. was trying to divert a little custom to his splendid new hotel down the road.

There were constant demands upon W.J.C.'s time apart from the day-to-day running of the Brewery. W.J.C. knew all about Public Relations even though the term had not been formally invented then.

Could the Licensee of the 'Belle Vue Inn' at Mansfield please hold two licences temporarily? Would Mr. Chadburn get it sorted out with Police Superintendent Tomasson? Would Mr. Chadburn attend to the improvement of the window light at the 'Ram Inn'? Would Mr. Chadburn attend to the 'Ram Inn' signboard that was encroaching over Mr. Renshaw's house? Would Mr. Chadburn investigate police complaints of betting in the Company's Inns? Would Mr. Chadburn deal with Mrs. Chadwick who has been convicted of an offence against the Licensing Laws at the 'Portland Arms', Sutton-in-Ashfield? Would Mr. Chadburn see tenants who were in arrears with their rent? Would Mr. Chadburn deal with Mr. Stead who has been convicted of an offence against the Licensing Laws at the 'Bell Hotel', Mansfield? Would Mr. Chadburn adjudicate regarding the rights in a wall between the 'Bird in Hand', Blidworth and the Vicarage? Would Mr. Chadburn inspect damage done to Brewery property at Skegby by coal miners on strike? Would Mr. Chadburn inspect the wall adjoining the 'Robin Hood Inn', Sutton-in-Ashfield? Would Mr. Chadburn do something about the sewer near the 'Apollo Tavern'? Would Mr. Chadburn consider new applicants for licences? Would Mr. Chadburn provide new closets in place of the old that had been destroyed by children? Would Mr. Chadburn see the sign that the rival brewers, Warwick of Newark, had erected in the archway of the 'Old Eclipse Inn'?

And so on and so on. In addition, of course, seldom a day passed without the need for W.J.C. to consider some addition, alteration, demands by Sanitary Inspectors for new drains, new toilets, almost every brick and tile of which needed Justices' Sanction, not to mention plans, plans and more plans.

It was an indication of the strength of W.J.C. that he surfaced above the sea of all these petty problems and not only concentrated his energies on continued expansion but had energy and interest to spare for municipal activities.

Only one partner, Shacklock, had been able to give him any regular administrative help and in 1899 he died. Hopewell was busy with his own affairs; Baily was enjoying almost daily drives around the Cornish countryside in carriages supplied by Thomas Warren, Job and Posting Master, 'Landaus, Phaetons and Other Carriages Always at Hand'. But Baily was not too indifferent to Brewery affairs to claim Shacklock's share in the

Alderman W. J. Chadburn (Mayor of Mansfield 1899)

business, available on his death.

There was bustle and excitement in the air as the world moved hopefully into the new century; although overshadowed somewhat by the anxieties of the Boer War, was this not also promising a tremendous upsurge locally in the mining industry known as the Boer War boom?

The new Cresswell Colliery had just been sunk and, a few years before, the Staveley Coal and Iron Company, a Derbyshire firm, had sunk the Warsop Colliery. There were plans by the proprietors of the Hucknall pits to sink the Sherwood Colliery in the Mansfield area. There was also a development by the coal mines to market the unwanted slack as coke and a number of collieries had installed coke ovens. The Pinxton Company joined up with the Coppeé Company of Belgium in installing fifty coke ovens.

Coal from which coke can be made is apparently only found in the Midlands area around Mansfield and not from the rest of the Leicestershire, Derbyshire and Nottinghamshire coalfield.

The coal owners of Nottinghamshire, Derbyshire and Leicestershire had always depended on the London trade which, in turn, depended upon the cost of transport. Sometimes the transport could cost as much as the coal.

It has been seen that the effect of the new railways upon canal traffic had achieved its greatest effect around 1855 when the Mansfield Brewery was founded. In that year coal traffic on the Grand Junction Canal was only about half of the quantity carried but five years before; and towards the end of the century the figure was dropping to below 5,000 tons from around the peak tonnage of 150,000.

It is assumed that canals in this country were killed by the railways and it may well be so; certainly it is true to the extent that the railways bought canals and then closed them. But had the canals been built wider, or rather the locks that, of course, controlled the maximum size of craft that could be used, they might have survived as the Continental canals have survived.

It is interesting to note that in 1896, when the battle with the railways had been all but lost, the Grand Junction Canal Company considered widening locks to increase the canal traffic from Nottinghamshire to London and particularly interesting because one of the methods decided upon was an Inclined Plane.

We created the Inclined Plane, used it for a few years and discarded it in 1910 as we allowed our waterway system to decay. The Belgians picked up our idea and created it into an Eighth Wonder of the World to fit in with their efficient inland waterway system of the 1970s. Ponder that as you sip your pint of Mansfield brew!

Whatever system was used to transport the coal, however, there was no doubt that trade was booming and naturally, prosperity for the mines meant prosperity for the Brewery which was barely able to keep up with the demand and the brewing capacity was severely strained, being maybe 400 or 500 barrels per week.

Although W. E. Baily increased his stake in the Brewery by buying the deceased Shacklock's share he showed not the slightest interest in the problems at Littleworth and W.J.C. battled on alone with the increasing frustrations and pressures of business. And not only did he carry the responsibilities of the Brewery single-handed but in that year he accepted the time consuming honour of becoming Mayor of Mansfield and led the town forward into the brave new century.

5

As the brewery entered the 20th century W. J. Chadburn could reflect that in his fifteen years in control he had gathered in more than fifty new public houses and hotels and he had negotiated loans in order to achieve this. The brewery owed over eighty thousand pounds and new and increased trade was needed to repay.

The buoyant new interest in drinking and socialising in public houses was countrywide and greater improvements were to be made to pubs during the first part of the 20th century than during the whole of the 19th century; and greater progress was made by W. J. Chadburn during his twenty most effective years than during the whole of the Brewery's preceding fifty years.

The trade was there for the taking, industry all around was expanding and W.J.C. realised that the brewery simply could not cope with the demand he had created, in its present form.

But he still managed to find time to promote progress locally as well. Trams were proposed for Mansfield and under the impressive title of the Light Railway Commission an enquiry was held on 1st June 1900 to consider an application from the promoters of a scheme of electrical tramways.

The Earl of Jersey and Colonel Boughey formed the commission which heard representations from Mr. Jesse Hind of Nottinghamshire County Council, Mr. J. Harrop White of Mansfield Town Council, Mr. J. D. Fidler of Sutton-in-Ashfield Urban District Council, Mr. C. F. Elliot Smith of Mansfield Woodhouse Urban District Council, Mr. William Jackson Chadburn, Mayor of Mansfield and many others.

It was proposed to have three lines emanating from the focal point of Market Place, Mansfield:

1. Due north to Mansfield Woodhouse for one and a half miles;
2. North-west along the Chesterfield Road for one mile and

3. South-west to Portland Square, Sutton-in-Ashfield, a distance of three and a quarter miles.

Quite largely as a result of W. J. Chadburn's interest, trams duly arrived in Mansfield.

The major event of 1901 was the death of Queen Victoria. In Mansfield W.J.C. was more concerned over the death of James Handley Hopewell, leaving Mr. Chadburn without a partner to discuss problems with although, naturally, the decision-making was invariably his. He had a partner, of course, but W. E. Baily went his indifferent way in Penzance. Not that his indifference had prejudiced his investment. The Mansfield Brewery Balance Sheet of 1901 showed Partners' Capital as:

W. E. Baily	£108,296. 6s. 11d.
Exors. of J. H. Hopewell	£27,074. 1s. 9d.
W. J. Chadburn	£27,074. 1s. 9d.

The Schedule of Freehold and Leasehold Properties at June 1901 numbered 44 fully licensed houses that were leasehold and 11 Freehold plus 17 beer houses.

There were many other shops with off-licences, fully licensed inns on short leaseholds, also beer houses and what were termed general properties.

Having recently bought Shacklock's share, W. E. Baily did not exercise his option to buy Hopewell's as well. He was shrewd enough to consider that the producer would work harder to serve his interest if he had a larger slice of the cake. W. J. Chadburn wrote to Baily in May 1901 that he was taking up Hopewell's share as Baily had failed to exercise his option to do so within the prescribed time limit set of two months. It was necessary for W.J.C. to mortgage almost every asset he could lay hands on in order to raise the necessary £27,000, the Brewery Deeds included.

While W.J.C. was engaged with the business of raising money, William Edward Baily was fully occupied at Penzance. When he was not driving in a one-horse carriage from his home, 'Lynwood', to the town and back at a cost of 10s., or to Marazion and back for 15s. plus 3s. 6d. for the driver, or engaging a carriage and pair to Land's End and back at a cost of 30s. plus 5s. for the driver, he was buying equipment for a new museum in the Paul district of Penzance.

He bought cabinets from T. Cooke and Son, Naturalists of Museum Street, who specialised in making cabinets for bird's eggs, insects, also entomological apparatus. He bought dozens of gelatine dry plates from Wratten and Wainwright, Photographic Chemists and Apparatus Makers of Great Queen Street, W.C. From Mr. A. C. Cossor, of Farringdon Road, E.C. he bought X-ray tubes and mercury. Needless to say he ignored all the bills sent to him for the supply of this equipment; in fact if all Mr. Cossor's accounts had proved so stubborn he might not have progressed to the commercial eminence he attained. He was still writing puzzled letters to the obdurate Mr. Baily two years after he had supplied him.

Admittedly there was not then the cash trade that we know today; indeed, tradesmen then appeared to find the sight of cash distasteful; the better class of customer they sought would have offended them by offering to pay for even the most humble purchase.

W. E. Baily's Ladyday Account with the local chemist brought forward an amount outstanding of £177. 2s. 6d. but went on adding to this formidable indebtedness with such trifles as 2 gals paraffin, 2s. nail brush, 6d.

His grocery order was never considered for payment until it had accumulated to over a hundred pounds but it grew faster than the bill of the chemist because it included a fortnightly delivery of 12 bottles of Begg's Whiskey and 12 bottles of Beaune or Corton, and in every other delivery there would be 12 bottles of port and 6 bottles of Wincarnis. The whiskey was 3s. 7d. a bottle; the Beaune and Corton, 5s. 6d.; the port, 6s. Soda syphons he bought thirty-six at a time.

It must be recorded that W. E. Baily was no stranger to the bottle. Even on their carriage drives through the Cornish countryside he would seek a little refreshment. They would stop the carriage at some country hotel and there would be half-crown teas for Mrs. Baily and the daughter Gertrude, a one-and-sixpenny tea for the driver but a bottle of Hiedsieck and brandy for Mr. Baily.

He was elected a country member of the Royal Societies Club. He was a member of the Royal Cornwall Polytechnic Society and his entry shows him as an F.L.S., F.Ent.Soc., and as a member of the Council, Geological Society, Cornwall.

To those of us who feel uncomfortable in making use of Club membership when our subscription remains unpaid, perhaps after three months or so from the due date, W. E. Baily appears as a record-holding defaulter. He happily continued his membership of clubs whose annual subscriptions he had not paid for six years. Yet after almost twenty years association with the Penzance district, by which time one might imagine that his reputation had preceded him in every direction, he was elected President of Paul Cricket Club.

He rented 'Lynwood' at Mousehole from about 1894 for £23.15s. a quarter and it was his home until his death. Although he did not return to Mansfield to live he did not sell his properties there – West Gate House and Farnsfield Farm – until 1902 and Baily's Horse, some of whom had lived there, were not paid off until then. The news of the sale of his Mansfield properties was sent by his solicitor to Mr. Baily at the largest resort hotel in the tropics; the Bailys were staying at the Marine Hotel, Barbados for the sake of his health. On this trip Mr., or more particularly Mrs., Baily met Mr. Walter Abbot who regularly wintered in Barbados.

Mrs. Baily did not enjoy Penzance; after her lively upbringing at the 'White Hart', Mansfield it must have been a dull existence for her, shut away for years in an isolated house in a secluded village at the very extremity of England. She had her daughter to keep her company it is true, but she does not appear to have been the brightest of children. The headmistress of St. Winifred's School, Clifton, Bristol had written to Mrs. Baily regretting that her daughter Gertrude Sarah would not be coming to the school, and regretting the cause.

On their return from Barbados the Bailys went for a short holiday to Worthing. After the stony beauty and isolation of Cornwall Mrs. Baily was enchanted with the soft freshness of the South Down; in addition, Mr. Walter Abbot lived there. They stayed at 'Warne's Hotel' on the front and left in October to return to winter in Cornwall; it was to be Mr. Baily's last.

William Edward Baily died on 26th May 1903 at Penzance. When the news was announced there was immediate interest and speculation amongst other breweries. The progress of William Jackson Chadburn had not gone unnoticed since his acquisitions had often been to the disadvantage of his competitors. Now, how was he faced financially?

The competition between brewers, though intense, was invariably of a friendly nature. The constitution of each other's partnerships and companies was no secret amongst the brewers in the area in which they operated. Details of finance naturally were. You visited your competitors and they visited you and you told each other everything and you told each other nothing in the nicest way.

The news was around in a flash to all competitors that William Jackson Chadburn was on his own. It would be known that he was over fifty years of age and that his sons were nowhere near old enough to take over; Francis, the eldest, was only 18 and said not to be in the best of health whilst Claude was only 16.

Besides, since William Edward Baily had been the original partner and was the senior partner it was obvious that there would be a majority shareholding to be picked up; even control perhaps? Was it not only a year or so back that another partner in Mansfield Brewery had died, requiring a settlement of his estate?

Expressions of sympathy at the death of his partner were received by W. J. Chadburn from neighbouring brewery chairmen. They added a postscript to the effect that if by any chance .....

Fortunately for W. J. Chadburn there was no such chance for any outsider. The Will of William Edward Baily might have been written by William Jackson Chadburn. It recognised the frailties of the Baily womenfolk and the astute business acumen of W. J. Chadburn, not to mention his absolute integrity. The vast amount of the Baily interest in the Brewery was left on trust for the benefit of his wife, Gertrude, and his only daughter, Gertrude Sarah; the Trustees were to be W. J. Chadburn and a Penzance solicitor, George Bodilly, and they were empowered to carry on 'his' brewery business in their absolute discretion as they should think fit.

They thought fit immediately to cast around for new partners since it was apparent to everyone that W.J.C. could not continue on his own, despite the fact that he had been virtually on his own for the last ten years.

It was eighteen years since Addison Titley had sold his half-share interest in the business but he was still around, indeed he was in the Brewery most days in connection with the malt supplies that he produced in his Midworth Street premises across the way.

It is not likely that Addison Titley would have cast envious eyes at the growing prosperity of the Mansfield Brewery for envy was not in his nature, besides which he was accumulating directorships in other directions. He still lived up at Gilcroft House but he was now 55 and not interested in returning to a partnership in the brewery that he had left almost twenty years earlier. But his eldest son showed interest; at the age of 28 he had read law at Cambridge and made a brief study of brewing but was still a little unsettled regarding the course of his career. He was close to his father and influenced by him. They had taken holidays together in Norway and France when the rest of the family had preferred to stay at home.

Edward Addison Titley decided to join the Mansfield Brewery as a partner. His next eldest brother, Walter, had set his heart upon conquering the New World but also allowed himself to be persuaded into becoming a partner in the brewery. One quarter of the Baily interest was sold to the Titleys and the new line-up of control appeared as:

The Trustees of William Edward Baily (William Jackson Chadburn and G. Bodilly)	six twelfths
William Jackson Chadburn	four twelfths
Edward Addison Titley	one twelfth
Walter Titley	one twelfth

It was agreed that W. J. Chadburn was to receive a salary of £1,000 per annum and the Titleys £200 per annum each.

When W. J. Chadburn had first come into the brewery he received £800 in his first year as did Shacklock and Hopewell; Baily received £2,400.

Over these first five years W. J. Chadburn's total rewards had worked out at £4,950. Shacklock and Hopewell had received the same amount but Baily, tucked away in Cornwall, had been sent £14,850.

In 1902, the year before Baily's death, Baily received £3,600 against Chadburn's £1,800. In the first full year of the new partnership following Baily's death the Titley brothers received £1,049; W. J. Chadburn £3,598 and the Baily womenfolk £5,510.

It so happened that this change of emphasis in the management of the company coincided closely with the development of the West Nottinghamshire coalfield as the quest for coal spread from the older Derbyshire pits to the east. In the Brewery's trading area the partners found a great new population growing up of dedicated beer drinkers and, where a few years before small wayside beer houses had satisfied the needs of the rural communities, now the resources of such cottage pubs were completely swamped by the new-rich customers. The first tentative rebuildings were the result, in the Kirkby, Sutton, Huthwaite, Pleasley and Woodhouse belt.

The new situation suited W. J. Chadburn ideally. There were big problems to be solved and a lot of money needed to be found but he had a completely free hand. The solicitor, Bodilly, knew as much about business as most solicitors of his day and was clearly of no account so far as the running of the brewery was concerned. In fact Bodilly's first suggestion to W.J.C. was that the business should be formed into a limited company. Mr. Chadburn considered it a most inopportune time to do so, explaining that as the brewery had operated as a private partnership for so many years with a partner like Mr. Baily the business was not in the right form to float as a company so soon after his death. Professional accountants had only been employed since 1900 and then principally as a result of Mr. Hopewell's death; prior to the turn of the century the Balance Sheet had been a very rough and ready affair. Also, the Wines, Spirits and Cigars Department was quite new, only having been introduced about the middle of 1902; it was a development capable of considerable expansion but no adequate price would be paid for this prospect by public subscription now. Money is scarce, W. J. Chadburn argued, and breweries are not at present looked upon with favour by the investing public as the state of the Licensing Law is so unsettled. Mr. Chadburn considered that a means should be found to tide over the present difficulty of obtaining money for the immediate wants of the Baily Estate.

Mr. Bodilly was clearly unhappy at the prospect of having been left by Mr. Baily with some responsibility for the conduct of a brewery but W. J. Chadburn was able to reassure him.

Next, Mr. Bodilly was niggling (in the way solicitors do when they cannot suggest any alternative), about the wisdom of bringing in the Titleys. W.J.C. rebuked him, saying that the Brewery were lucky indeed to have the interest of a family with such influence and command of capital.

A valuation in connection with the recent sorting out of Hopewell's Estate had revealed that the Brewery assets were worth £238,321. Loans and mortgages owing amounted to £69,262 and there was an overdraft at Samuel Smith's Bank of £15,537.

The old and the new. The 'Dial Hotel', Mansfield and the 'Pike and Heron', Sheffield

6

The Victorian Age came to an end in 1901 but the confidence that it had created continued as an influence. At the turn of the century Britain led the world and its society, freed from Victorian stodginess, stepped out into the Edwardian era to enjoy themselves. It was a time of peace and pleasure and prosperity.

But discord was growing beneath the surface. Lloyd George was criticising the conduct of the Boer War, the Government were building big new battleships – Dreadnoughts – to discourage the naval ambitions of Germany; and Germany was widening the Kiel Canal to allow her big ships through. The diplomatic poker game had worldwide implications. A long way away, much too far away to worry about, Russia and Japan engaged in a war on their own.

Trade Unions were growing in power and influence. There were three Labour members in the House of Commons but with hopes of party power so remote that they were seeking alliance with the Liberals.

Of more importance to W. J. Chadburn and the Titleys were the disputes that had arisen since Gladstone's licensing of public houses. Even where there was no evidence of any trouble the licensing authorities were refusing the annual renewals here and there, sometimes simply because it was considered that there were too many public houses in an area. To the Liberal Nonconformists one public house was one too many. The Licensing Act of 1904 was introduced to provide compensation where licences were taken away on grounds other than misconduct. The compensation was paid from a fund raised by the brewers and the drink trade generally.

At the time of writing it is still in being and the present Chairman of the Brewery is directly involved in national discussions about its winding up.

Despite these problems in the country at large the demand

for Mansfield Ale increased continually and it was becoming increasingly apparent to W. J. Chadburn and the Titleys that the productive capacity of the Brewery would have to be increased, even if it meant building another brewery. In considering these problems W. J. Chadburn was comforted to have the interest and concern of Edward Addison Titley who took his duties as a Partner most conscientiously; more so, indeed, than his younger brother, Walter, whose greatest delight was in travelling around in the Brewery gig.

A regular tour of the public houses was necessary for the collection of rents and beer monies due and the appointed servants, whose duty this was, soon came to regard with apprehension the appearance of Mr. Walter in the gig. If, on these occasions, they returned without mishap they were fortunate indeed; it was too much to hope that their money would be fully accounted for since Mr. Walter was a great believer in public relations and enjoyed spending in one pub what he had collected at the last. Although he overturned the gig on many occasions he never lost his enthusiasm for the collecting journey. The same could not be said for his travelling companions who quite often preferred to walk on these occasions and thought nothing of going on their collecting rounds to Edwinstowe on foot, a distance there and back of fourteen miles.

It is taken for granted that all progress is beneficial, even necessary. And it may be so, but what charm life must have held when it was part of one's job to tread the paths of Robin Hood through Sherwood Forest. Occasionally, if the weather was unkind, they would travel on the carrier's cart.

In due course Mr. Walter succumbed to boredom and his ambition to conquer the New World. He left for Canada. His younger brothers also sought their fortunes abroad, Samuel in Ceylon and Basil in Australia.

Their father, Addison Titley, sold Gilcroft House, Mansfield and went to live at Duffield Bank House, Derbyshire, in 1904.

Edward Addison Titley, unmarried at the age of 29, came to the brewery each day from his home at Chilwell.

W. J. Chadburn was living at Grove House (the property of the Duke of Portland), just up the hill from the Brewery and half-way to the Malting premises in Midworth Street. From his bedroom window he could see the Brewery lying below. In those days founders of businesses usually lived on or near their factories; however unpleasant the environment it took second place to the more important consideration of making money. They worked long hours but not on Sundays for then streets were deserted, shops were shut and churches were well attended. (So, fortunately for Mansfield Brewery, were the pubs.)

W. J. Chadburn would walk down from Grove House at 7 a.m. and naturally everybody would be there before him and all work in progress. He would go back for breakfast at about 9 a.m., then for lunch at 12.30 and for tea at 4.30, after which he would continue working at the brewery.

The brewery employees worked hard too, but once a year W.J.C. would send them off on their annual outing by charabanc, perhaps to the Dukeries or into Derbyshire. W.J.C. never joined them. They would set off from Littleworth with the driver blowing his horn; it was an age of simple pleasures and the outing was eagerly anticipated. Afterwards, the smallest happening would be recalled many times over and one great event was never forgotten by anyone who witnessed it; on that occasion the lead horse of the charabanc got a foot over the trace and they finished up in Boots' window in Leeming Street.

Refreshed by their outing the employees would return to meet the ever-increasing demand for the Mansfield Brew. Due to this incessant and continuing demand for more beer they were no doubt in difficulty in supplying the increased call.

The beginning of the 20th century was a period of intense political activity directed against the drink trade and great changes were taking place in the structure of the trade as a whole. By and large the companies which survived this period and the subsequent upheaval of the Great War were those whose management had sufficient courage and vision to see further than their current frustrations and difficulties. William Jackson Chadburn was one of these.

The great decision was made to build a new brewery. The Partners were spurred on in their decision by the damning contents of a technical report on the condition of the old brewery by the eminent Chaston Chapman, one of the most erudite of the 19th century practical scientists. His report categorically insisted that unless the Partners started again – afresh – they might as well give up brewing.

This is not such an indictment of the Partners' management ability as it may appear at first sight. To a greater or less degree breweries built in the previous century were in much the same structural condition as Mansfield. They had been built before Pasteur published his revolutionary thesis 'Etudes sur la bierè' and pointed the way to some measure of biological control in the production of beer.

Fortunately for the trade at about this time an architect, Stovin Bradford, was devoting himself to the rebuilding of such premises with conspicuous skill and success. He was a man of great practical experience and foresight since many of the breweries he designed are still brewing successfully and economically, and by reason of their forward-looking design have been readily adapted to modern practices. Bradford's Breweries were all crowned by his trade mark of a decorative railed parapet with a flagpole.

W. J. Chadburn and Edward Addison Titley resolved that they would plough back profits in order to pay back mortgages, to reduce the bank overdraft and to find the money to build the new brewery needed to cope with their growing trade. They hoped to persuade Mrs. Baily and Gertrude to do the same, a not unreasonable assumption since mother and daughter could not possibly have any real need for the large sums of money that the Brewery was paying them each year in profits.

Miss Gertrude Baily attained her majority in May 1905 after which the Trustees, Bodilly and W. J. Chadburn, were no longer required to handle her affairs. In fact, by then the Bailys had moved away from Bodilly's influence; indeed within weeks of her husband's death Mrs. Baily was planning to get away from the desolation of the house at Penzance to the more sophisticated environment of Worthing.

W. J. Chadburn might well have reckoned upon being the sole guide, philosopher and friend to the Baily womenfolk in advising them how best to invest the considerable profits they received from the brewery. But six months after Gertrude came of age her mother married again, becoming Mrs. Walter Abbot in September 1905. This intelligence must have caused W.J.C. some apprehension since his need for re-investment of the Baily profits was critical to his plans for the progress of the brewery. On one point, however, perhaps on the main point, he had no cause for concern. Walter Abbott was no adventurer but a very considerable business man in his own right. The Abbotts were proprietors of the Saxone and Sorosis Shoe Company of 57, Strand and eighteen branches; he was to become a good friend of W.J.C. in the problems ahead. At the beginning his ability to compare investment yields with those the brewery offered was not always appreciated.

Mr. Walter Abbott introduced the Baily womenfolk to a regular style of existence more in keeping with their income, a style that they had only glimpsed when sharing life with the late lamented Commander of Baily's Horse. Baily took them to hotels for half-crown teas; Abbott took them for weeks to a suite at the St. Ermins Hotel simply to shop in London, even inviting friends, including the Chadburn family, to join them as their guests.

Baily took them on one occasion to Barbados for a fortnight's holiday; Abbott had wintered there regularly for the past sixteen years.

But Abbott needed little or nothing of their Mansfield Brewery monies and he could see the wisdom of their re-investing back into the Brewery any surplus to their requirements. His business was secure and he could see that money ploughed back to buy another hotel or public house, or to help build a new brewery, was compounding their profit earning potential very considerably.

In 1906 W.J.C. and Edward Addison Titley pressed ahead with their plans to build the new brewery. Also in this year Claude, W.J.C.'s second son, came to work at the Brewery. He was nineteen years of age and his father was tolerant in allowing him to do much as he pleased. Francis, too, came to the Brewery when his health allowed but the boys were not required to keep to their father's routine. In any case Francis was more interested in engineering than in brewing.

Sometimes the boys would hand out the daily ration of beer from the small cellar by the front office, sometimes Tommy Gilbert dispensed it, sometimes the men helped themselves. They would come in from the yard with a can or jug and if there was no one there to serve them Mr. Titley would call to them to serve themselves but to keep whistling while they were filling their can. (It is impossible to sup ale while whistling!)

From their beds the boys would watch W.J.C. set off from Grove House at 7 a.m. each morning and it would be a scramble for them to be ready at the time he returned for his breakfast.

Claude's most important contribution to the life of the Brewery was in playing for the Mansfield Brewery Football team. Apart from this he watched and noted the stresses and strains to which his father and Edward Addison Titley were subject and undoubtedly these experiences influenced the way he came to play his hand when he eventually took control.

On a national level this was the year that The Labour Representation Committee adopted the title of The Labour Party. Following the General Election of 1906 there were 29 Labour M.P.'s and 25 Lib-Labs, of whom 13 were miners.

The rebuilding of the brewery would need so much money that it was obvious to W.J.C. and Edward Titley that they should seek the cooperation of Walter Abbott in order that he could influence the Baily womenfolk as necessary. Accordingly W.J.C. prepared a statement of the present values of brewery properties and mortgage details:

29 properties valued at £78,300 were charged to The Union of London and Smith's Bank to secure the share of	£27,000 held in the business by W.J.C.
19 properties were similarly held to secure an overdraft/loan of	£45,000
33 properties were mortgaged to various private individuals and trustees.	
22 properties were free of mortgage.	

Walter Abbott appreciated the need for the new brewery and promised to help in persuading his wife and Gertrude to plough back whatever share of profits W.J.C. thought reasonable. Whatever share of profits W.J.C. asked the Baily womenfolk to plough back he and Edward Titley always accepted that a similar proportion of their own profits should be lent back to the business.

Chadburn and Titley had, in fact, ploughed back into the business by way of loans quite a large proportion of their annual share of profits and they had experienced no difficulty in persuading Mr. and Mrs. Abbott and Miss Baily to do the same. The bank, as is their habit, were always pressing for a reduction in the Brewery overdraft, mortgages were falling due for repayment, properties needed alteration and repair, there

Changes in Mansfield. The 'King's Head' on Stockwell Gate now adjoins the Town's Central Shopping Precinct.

were always temptations in the way of properties to buy and now, of course, the new brewery was to be built. Profits were declared in February or March based on the previous year end figures. If Miss Baily was to receive £5,000 in a year W.J.C. would ask her to lend back £3,000 on which he paid her interest; even the balance of £2,000 left to her was excessive for her simple needs.

In February 1907 when her mother and Walter Abbott were wintering in Barbados as usual W.J.C. wrote his usual 'Dear Gertrude', 'Yours affectionately' letter to Miss Baily asking for the £3,000 that she had promised but not sent. Eventually he received a frosty reply from a solicitor called Verrall requiring to know what deeds were to be charged against the £3,000 requested from Miss Baily, also what were the details of the properties and where was the evidence of the value of them.

W.J.C. was probably ready with his paying-in slip to pay in Gertrude's cheque and would certainly have had precedents for assuring his bank manager that her £3,000 would be forthcoming almost before she had banked her share-of-profits cheque from which the £3,000 was to come.

No one could criticise his concern for his client but by his attitude and delay Verrall was to raise the blood pressure of the Brewery Partners on many occasions; on this introductory matter of the urgently needed £3,000, for instance, he let the Brewery know just where they stood in his scale of priorities by informing them that he had been much too busy to go into the matter of the £3,000. Brushing off W.J.C.'s protest at the delay Verrall accounted for it by brazenly explaining that he had put the Brewery letter in his pocket.

When Mr. Chadburn patiently supplied evidence that the security for Miss Baily's loan was 'The Old Spot Inn' and two cottages at Pleasley plus 'The White Swan' at Mansfield Woodhouse, all valued at a figure in excess of £6,500, Verrall wanted to know the trade done at each public house. He added, stiffly, that he would have preferred some different security to licensed premises. This to a brewery company!

The plans had been settled early in 1907 for the building of the new brewery and the Partners needed all the money they could get. W.J.C. felt perfectly justified in asking the Bailys for as much as they could spare since they would be the principal beneficiaries from the increased profits that the new brewery would produce.

W.J.C. thought that it might help to explain all this in a long letter to Verrall; a fortnight later he enquired if Verrall had received his letter. The solicitor replied that he had been too busy to go into the matter but that he could not release Miss Baily's £3,000, that was lying idle, because he was not satisfied with the security offered.

Mr. Chadburn sent him the deeds of the Blind Lane Malt-kilns. Verrall took a fortnight to reply that he was not satisfied which was more than William Jackson Chadburn could stand. He instructed Verrall to return all the deeds and that he would make alternative arrangements; he would not require Miss Baily's money, despite the fact that the rebuilding of the new brewery was being undertaken with the knowledge and concurrence of Mr. and Mrs. Abbott and Miss Baily and upon the strength of their promises to lend substantial sums towards the cost. W.J.C. concluded, ominously, that he would lose no time in seeing Mr. Abbott on his return.

Verrall capitulated and was not then too busy to attend to the matter of Miss Baily's cheque which he sent immediately. Gertrude, of course, was unaware of the delay he had caused; in any case she was fully engaged in the building of her own house at Worthing.

When, a month or so later, Mr. Abbott was back at Worthing, he wrote to W.J.C. enquiring if the £3,000 was sufficient. Surely, he added, £6,000 had been promised.

Throughout the summer of 1907 the building of the brewery proceeded. The cost of it was estimated at £15,000 which W.J.C. and Edward Titley aimed to pay out of income despite the need to alter and rebuild several public houses to meet the requirements of the Licensing Justices.

In the Brewery itself there were changes taking place at the very heart of the enterprise, changes revolutionising the quality of the Mansfield Brew without which all other expenditure would have been to no avail. New, gleaming slate fermenting vessels were installed to take the place of the old double stone walled containers that had done service for fifty years or more; these unhygienic vessels were enough to guarantee the sourness of any brew entrusted to them, quite apart from the other hazards of rats and snails.

W.J.C. wrote again to Gertrude asking for £3,000 and also expressing the hope that The Ladies would pay proportionate amounts out of their incomes towards the brewery rebuilding.

Do you mean in addition to the £3,000 already sent? replied Mr. Abbott; if so, I think that that is asking a great deal in one year.

Financial problems were beginning to get W.J.C. down. Certainly I mean an additional £3,000, he replied to Mr. Abbott, taking exception to the tone of his enquiry. He went on that if Mr. Abbott could not advise The Ladies to share with W.J.C. and Edward Titley their proportionate burdens then it would be necessary to sell licensed properties to raise money, the effect of which would be disastrous.

Mr. Abbott gently suggested to W.J.C. that Gertrude's income must be treated as her own private property; whatever she loans to the business must be in the nature of a loan as from a stranger.

The strain was telling on Mr. Chadburn and he decided to go away. In addition to the problems of the Brewery his eighteen-year-old eldest son, Francis, was ill with consumption and then, of course, the medical world had no answer to this progressive wasting disease.

W.J.C. was fortunate to be able to leave the rebuilding, and the affairs of the Brewery, in the capable hands of Edward Addison Titley, now thirty-two years of age and still unmarried.

The brewery was completed. Walter Abbott wrote in the most friendly fashion inviting W.J.C. to come out to the West Indies with him. After two winters in Barbados, he explained, his wife had decided to remain with Gertrude in Worthing. Mr. Abbott explained that he had instructed Verrall regarding the amounts to be refunded to the Brewery from profits but asked W.J.C. to appreciate that the difficulties Verrall created were not of Abbott's making.

At this time Edward Titley was telling Verrall that he had no intention of providing him with £12,000 of security to cover a loan of £3,000 by Miss Baily. W.J.C. returned to the fray. If we send you our cheque for Miss Baily's share of profits will you undertake to send us her £3,000 by return? he enquired of Verrall who replied to enquire how much were the profits.

Before he could attend to this W.J.C. was called away to be with Francis who had taken a turn for the worse. It was left to Edward Titley to inform Verrall that Miss Baily's share of profits was £8,686 but it was not the solicitor's style to be impressed with anything that an East Midlands brewery might achieve.

Assuming that the amount correctly represents the share due to Miss Baily, he replied acidly, he would, on receipt of the £8,686, send the £3,000.

The Ladies were impressed with the results however, in fact Mr. Abbott wrote from the West Indies that The Ladies were delighted with the results. From his peaceful hide-away at the 'Constant Spring Hotel', St. Andrew, Jamaica, Walter Abbott regretted that Verrall was adding to the problems of the Partners in Mansfield.

7

In 1906, the year before the new brewery was built the trade was 17,000 barrels; in 1908, the year after, the trade amounted to 20,000 barrels.

The increase in trade was so dramatic at certain premises that one can only assume that some form of rationing was imposed prior to the increase in production provided by the new Brewery. Landlords may have been tempted to open for longer hours once they knew that increased supplies were assured because, of course, there were no licensing hours then.

The nearest public house to the Brewery was the 'Ram Inn' at Littleworth; so near, in fact, that the Brewery windows overlooked it. It was kept by a widow, Harriet Reynolds Jarvis, who had moved there in December 1906. Previously she had lived at the 'Black Bull' where her husband, Harry Jarvis Senior, was the landlord. They left the 'Black Bull' in January 1906 to move to the 'Ram Inn' but he died before he could take up his new duties and the licence was granted in the name of his widow.

At the time she moved to the 'Ram Inn, Harriet Jarvis had two children, Harry aged 7 and Evelyn Jessie aged 4.

The Partners of the Brewery were in the habit of visiting their licensed premises, as the directors are now, and Harriet Reynolds Jarvis attracted the attention of Edward Addison Titley who was then thirty-one years of age.

The new Brewery was built and nearly paid for, W.J.C. having sold a row of cottages in Leeming Street and other property to help raise the money. It says a great deal for Mr. Chadburn's courage and faith in the future to carry through such an ambitious venture in the face of fierce criticism. He was fifty-five years of age and was by no means completely certain then how Edward Addison Titley was going to turn out, particularly as Edward's attentions were so much engaged at that time with the widow Jarvis of the 'Ram Inn'.

Anyhow, it was a fine modern brewhouse and the old museum was adapted to house the fermenting room. One feature of the new brewhouse was the adequate room provided to manoeuvre round all the vessels, and adequate height overall so that the working conditions were ideal. It was built by Percival of Mansfield who, later in 1938, was to build much more of the extensions then required. The tiling was a feature of the construction and it was much ahead of its day. The brewing department were later of the opinion that W.J.C. stopped short of some of the things he should have done but there was not the appreciation of the need for sterility in 1906. The plant was, of course, designed around the horse and cart.

It is difficult to estimate what the capacity of the 1854 brewery was but it could have been about 500 barrels a week. It was replaced by a plant capable of an output of 650 barrels a week with room in the fermenting room for installation of another 150 barrels capacity. Fermentation was divided into some 4 × 25 brl. vessels, 12 × 33 brl. vessels and 3 × 150 brl. vessels.

It is not known, and it is difficult to guess, whether in designing the 1906 brewhouse Bradford was working to an overall plan which envisaged future modernisation, incorporating those parts of the brewery he did not touch; but whether by accident or design the central core he erected has, over the years, formed the nucleus of all future developments. The levels were right, the grouping of the vessels was right and extensions have fallen readily into place. Logical development has been easy.

With the brewery completed it was necessary to attack the money problems that the building of it had created. The bank never ceased their cry for reduction of the overdraft. The Partners decided to trim this by disposing of all non-licensed properties. Over the years, in buying licensed premises they had picked up odd adjoining cottages and buildings and pieces of land that could now be usefully turned into money. These unwanted bits and pieces were included in the deeds of the principal properties and needed to be legally disentangled for separate sale. This meant seeking Gertrude Sarah's permission, which she gave immediately.

She thanked Mr. Chadburn for some money and expressed delight at the photographs of the new brewery. She appeared to be more concerned to enquire affectionately after the state of

Francis's health; and to tell Mr. Chadburn excitedly about her mother's new little motor-car that held two in front and one behind; and that although mother had only had it for a week she had learned to drive it already although, of course, she had not been out without the chauffeur. As for the sale of the properties she was perfectly content to rely upon Mr. Chadburn as her Trustee.

Not so Verrall. Is Miss Baily's security affected? he demanded. No, replied W.J.C. Verral persisted that he relied upon W.J.C. to sell nothing affecting Miss Baily's security and to prove how much he relied upon Mr. Chadburn he then requested a plan showing exactly what had been sold.

The properties realised £5,000 and the bank loan was reduced by this amount. Yet a few months later, when Walter Abbott wrote to ask if they could have their October instalment a month early as the three of them were leaving to winter in Jamaica, W.J.C. asked them to defer paying in the £300 each he sent them as the bank were again pressing him for money.

Francis Chadburn was cordially invited to join the party on this occasion as it was thought that a winter in the West Indies would benefit his health. His doctor, however, would not allow him to make the sea passage and instead he spent two months with his mother at Bridlington.

Meanwhile Edward Addison Titley was seeing a lot of Harriet Jarvis at the 'Ram Inn'. You will remember that since his father and mother had moved to Duffield a few years ago he had lived on his own at Chilwell.

The trade resulting from the new brewery was good and it was hoped that the profits would be sufficient to finish paying for it. From Gertrude's share she agreed in advance to hand back another £3,000 bringing the amount paid back by her in the preceding three years to £12,000. W.J.C. had matched this in proportion with £9,000 and Edward Addison Titley with £7,000.

The following year Walter Abbott had completed arrangements for visiting Barbados on his own but, at the last moment, his wife decided to join him, very much against his, and her daughter's, wishes. Mrs. Abbott was invariably made utterly miserable and ill by the steamship voyages that her husband loved so well. (The quality of first-class shipboard life was then at a peak of perfection and who amongst those who enjoyed such luxury could have imagined that such days were numbered, for Blériot had made his first cross-Channel flight in July 1909.) Apart from the fact that the voyage made her miserable it seems that life in Barbados was not entirely to Mrs. Abbott's liking for Sarah was summoned to Barbados three months after her mother sailed because she was so lonely there. Gertrude and Walter Abbott had then been married for four years. He was keen to take W.J.C.'s eldest son as his companion but Francis did not appear to be any more enthusiastic about the sea voyage than his doctor and he spent much of the year on the East Coast, and some time in Switzerland.

Despite the many problems engaging his attention, W.J.C. was still alive to the progress and opportunities occurring outside the world of brewing. The Act incorporating the Mansfield Railway Company was dated 26th July 1910 and the capital of £250,000 was raised in £10 shares. The first Directors numbered seven and one of them was William Jackson Chadburn. At this time a move had been launched locally to attract the Great Central Railway to Mansfield and to provide competition to the Midland Railway monopoly; also to provide a quicker route to the coast by the East–West Railway – Sheffield–Cleethorpes and the Lincolnshire coast. The Midland Railway was adequately serving the mineral trade. W.J.C. was interested in this scheme and was made chairman of the organising committee. The route chosen through the town passed along the edge of the Meadows, now Tichfield Park, an open space previously given to the town by the Duke of Portland. From Mansfield Brewery point of view the worst feature of the scheme was that W.J.C. sold the land at the back of the brewery along the line of what was to become Great Central Road. At the time it must have looked like so much surplus grazing land. Who could at that time have envisaged the present scene, with every square foot of it covered by buildings and roadways. It is a sobering thought that W.J.C.'s grandson would be re-purchasing the land and expanding on to it within so short a time, the life of the railway having run its full course in 60 years.

In 1910 Walter Abbott got away early in August to Barbados but proposed to return for his wife in January. He was glad to report that Gertrude was at last taking a little interest in her own affairs and getting away from the influence of Verrall. Naturally this was of the greatest interest to W.J.C. because the Baily ladies were continually being urged to lend back substantial amounts of the profits paid to them in order to reduce the Brewery indebtedness to the bank.

In 1910 Edward Addison Titley married Harriet Jarvis and she left the 'Ram Inn'. With her children, now aged eleven and nine they first went to live at West Bridgford whilst looking for a house but finally settled at Chilwell where Edward Titley had lived during his bachelor days. He came to the brewery every day by train, walking to Beeston Station and changing at Nottingham for Mansfield. So regular was he in his habits and so punctual the trains that you could set your watch to a quarter-to-ten as you sighted him walking down the hill.

He and W. J. Chadburn had been running the Brewery for nine years when Mr. Chadburn decided that the time was opportune to admit his sons to a share of the partnership. W. J. Chadburn was sixty-two when a new Partnership Agreement was signed and the new shareholding arrangement was:

Trustee of William Edward Baily (W. J. Chadburn was the sole surviving trustee)	six twelfths
William Jackson Chadburn	two twelfths
Edward Addison Titley	two twelfths
Francis Ludlow Chadburn	one twelfth
Claude Chadburn	one twelfth

It was agreed that Mr. Chadburn and Edward Titley should manage the business and that Mr. Chadburn's sons should assist. W.J.C. received a salary of £1,000 a year, Edward Titley £600 and the sons £200 each.

At about this time W. J. Chadburn moved from Grove House to Nettleworth Manor and he now preferred to travel in to work in his chauffeured car in preference to the Brewery gig.

The brewery trade settled back somewhat after the splendid surge following the building of the new brewery, one reason being the National Coal Strike of 27th February 1912 when every colliery in the country was at a standstill. The strike was over a guaranteed minimum wage and it lasted until March when Prime Minister Asquith's Government introduced a Minimum Wage Bill. As a result the profits for the year were down and early in 1913 W.J.C. could send Gertrude only

£4,826 of which he wanted £3,000 back as a further loan. It was enough to send her back to Verrall who immediately demanded a statement of the total amounts lent by each partner, plus a statement of the amount owing to the bank, plus a balance sheet. He also inspired a statement from Gertrude that she had invested quite enough of her savings in the Brewery; she wanted to make other investments with her money.

Verrall was told that the total loans were: Gertrude £24,000, W. J. Chadburn £19,000, Edward Addison Titley £11,000. In the last five years the Brewery had reduced its bank loans from £45,000 to the present figure of £22,000.

W.J.C. did not take up with Gertrude her desire to invest her money outside of the Brewery. For the time being he had had enough of coping with the daily worries of the Brewery, the constant niggling of the bank, Gertrude's surprising show of independence prompted, no doubt, by the unsympathetic Verrall. Leaving Edward Titley in charge he went off to the South of France and when he returned Verrall was dead.

W.J.C. had drafted a letter to Gertrude hoping that she would continue to invest as she had in past years and adding, in the nicest way, that if she did not put her money back into the Brewery neither would he or Mr. Titley. Gertrude replied that she would let him know.

A few months later he invited her to come and stay at Nettleworth Manor. She declined on the grounds that her mother was alone in the absence of Mr. Abbott in the West Indies. Would not Mr. and Mrs. Chadburn and Francis like to come and stay with them at Worthing? W.J.C. declined, pleading ill health, coupled with the need for his presence at the Brewery during an exceptionally busy time. There were other interests too. He was as fascinated with railways and their development as were many businessmen of his time and his shareholding in the Mansfield Railway and its progress gave him much satisfaction.

The section of the Mansfield Railway from Mansfield Colliery to Clipstone opened on 13th June 1913 and from Mansfield Colliery to Mansfield on 2nd June 1914. The remaining section from Kirkby to Mansfield was not finished until 4th September 1916.

The 1914 profits cheque was sent to Gertrude by Claude Chadburn as W.J.C. was away ill. Gertrude offered half by way of an additional loan. Edward Titley wrote to tell her that the profits for the year ending December 1913 amounted to £27,159 of which her share was £5,589 as she had drawn already £1,200 on account. Would she not make her additional loan a round sum of £3,000? Gertrude explained that when she spoke of investing half she meant half of her usual £3,000, or £1,500, but she agreed to increase this to £2,000.

Claude Chadburn was married and, shortly afterwards, was called up in the South Notts Hussars.

At the beginning of the First World War Asquith's Liberal Cabinet included Lloyd George as Chancellor of the Exchequer, Earl Kitchener as Secretary for War and Winston Churchill as First Lord of the Admiralty.

When the war had been in progress for a month or so Mr. Chadburn wrote to tell Gertrude that it was adversely affecting trade although, in the beginning it was widely expected that the war would be over in a few weeks. But the weeks went by and it did not end. The railways were taken over by the Government. Chancellor Lloyd George issued paper pound notes to take the place of gold sovereigns.

Yet early in 1915 Mr. Chadburn was able to write his usual 'Dear Gertrude', 'Yours affectionately' letter telling her that the Brewery was now doing well despite the war. Into the Mansfield Brewery area had come an Army Camp of sixty thousand men at Clipstone; a special railway station had been built for them giving added importance to the Mansfield Railway and to the area. In addition to this the coal mines were expanding. The North Shaft had been sunk at Kirkby, also the Lowmoor Shaft and the Rufford Shaft. W.J.C. told Gertrude that he was most anxious to reduce the Brewery indebtedness to the bank and hoped that she would leave in £3,000 when she received her next profits cheque. She replied that she proposed putting all her money into war Loan. Verrall had been succeeded by his son and W.J.C. could easily imagine that Gertrude had been influenced; her share of profits was nearly £6,000 and it was unlike her to spare nothing for the Brewery.

She most certainly had been influenced but not by Verrall. She had a new adviser now, a husband, but she kept this secret from W.J.C. despite the fact that they had shared a family closeness for all of her thirty-one years and despite the fact that W.J.C. had been her Trustee since the death of her father twelve years before.

W.J.C. addressed his letters to Miss Gertrude Baily and she

did not correct him; he told her that although he appreciated her patriotism he had recently been obliged to turn down the offer of a good hotel that her usual loan would have bought.

Verrall Junior wrote to W.J.C. on routine tax matters relating to Miss Gertrude Baily although he had already drawn up her marriage settlement in her new married name.

It was not until nine months after her marriage that Verrall wrote to W.J.C. enclosing formal notices of Miss Baily's new status as Mrs. Thomas and her marriage settlement. Understandably W.J.C. was surprised, probably a little hurt that after all the years Gertrude had not confided in him. He would certainly rather have heard the news from her than from Verrall: as it was he had to enquire who the lucky fellow was and the solicitor told him that he was a Lieutenant in the Army, home on leave having been wounded. Thus Gertrude's patriotism no doubt; it explained her refusal to hand back any of her last share of profits which might also be seen as a straw in the wind regarding the prospect of future loans from her. In any case, if the fellow had no money she would probably need the whole of her income. The major part of her loans to the Brewery she had settled upon him as a Marriage Settlement. Lieutenant Thomas was a lucky man financially.

However, trade was increasing and the rush of business had somehow to be coped with by a much reduced staff since a number of employees were now in the Forces. The pointing finger of Kitchener on the widely distributed posters brought in two million men under arms in a matter of months. (There were to be five million engaged before the war was over.)

The Defence of the Realm Act imposed limited opening hours for licensed houses amongst other restrictions. In the year that D.O.R.A. was introduced it would be imagined that the sales of beer would have fallen dramatically; in fact the limiting of hours was not noticed because beer had already been rationed for some time and it was not unusual for pubs to be closed for days on end through lack of supplies.

In addition to rationing beer it had also been diluted by order.

Although trade might have been a lot worse for the Brewery, money was difficult, the bank was still owed a lot of money and now W.J.C. could see that Gertrude's help was going to be withdrawn. This new Lieutenant Thomas fellow might even want repayment of her loans.

William Jackson Chadburn was now sixty-five and assailed by more problems than he had ever been called upon to face in his life. At the end of 1915 he had his first serious illness and it was nearly three months before he could again attend to business matters.

8

Early in the year Edward Titley was trying to cope on his own as W. J. Chadburn was still away ill and, in fact, his condition was now causing concern. There was a lot of business to attend to and the staff was depleted.

In January 1916 the Military Service Act came into force making unmarried men between eighteen and forty-five liable to be called up; entry into the Armed Forces had been voluntary until then. There were exceptions to conscription, including coal miners whose patriotic voluntary enlistment had caused manpower problems in the industry.

At the Brewery Edward Titley was being pressed by the bank to reduce the overdraft and he had to pin his hopes on receiving some help from Gertrude again this year.

Instead he received a request from Verrall for repayment of two of Gertrude's mortgages amounting to £6,000. He told Verrall that it was most inconvenient and Verrall replied that it was his last wish to cause the Brewery any inconvenience.

Encouraged by the withdrawal of Gertrude's request Edward Titley then wrote to her asking if she would leave another £3,000 in as an additional loan out of her share of profits about to be paid to her. Edward Titley was clearly overworked and not in the mood for feather-bedding the Baily interests; he reminded Gertrude that she and her mother owned a half of the Brewery yet it was Mr. Chadburn and he who had to work tremendously hard in troubled times to obtain the results.

Gertrude took a fortnight to reply and then wrote from Plymouth formally regretting that she could not see her way clear to make any further advance. The arrival of her letter at the Brewery coincided with Mr. Chadburn's return to work. Having suffered quite a severe stroke he had been warned by his doctor to take things more easily and to observe a careful diet.

He ignored both directions, eating large steaks of which he was fond and working harder than ever.

He wrote to Gertrude immediately but it was 'Dear Mrs. Thomas', 'Yours sincerely' now. He had not forgiven her for keeping her marriage secret from him and she was never to be 'Dear Gertrude', 'Yours affectionately' again. He sent her £5,675 and said that the Partners would leave in proportions of their profits if she would do the same. He may have been bluffing because the bank would have required the Partners' proportions to be left in anyway. However, Gertrude sidestepped the responsibility of offending Mr. Chadburn by passing the matter to Verrall.

Verrall left W.J.C. in no doubt about Gertrude not lending any more but he asked for details and was told that Mr. and Mrs. Chadburn, their two sons and Mr. Titley had left in £41,000 against Gertrude's £26,000; also that the bank overdraft was £17,000.

Verrall decided that the best way of solving the problem was to do nothing, a practice that seems to suit the legal profession better than industry. After two months Edward Titley sent him a reminder and told him that the partners had left in £6,500 despite W.J.C.'s threat to Gertrude that they would not. Verrall offered £1,000 if Gertrude – or Mrs. Thomas as she was now known – could have more security and asked for a lot of information regarding the Trust securities. Edward Titley was too busy to look out the information required and he pointed out to Verrall that the Brewery staff was depleted owing to members having joined the Colours; Verrall reminded him that the Brewery was not singular in this respect. The months went by. No money was sent by Verrall.

Trade was down somewhat but was holding a great deal better than it was in some parts of the country. The development to its full potential of the Mansfield coal mining area had been interrupted by shortages of skilled labour and materials. In the first eighteen months of the war more than twenty-five thousand miners had voluntarily joined up, and they were, of course, the cream of the mining industry, the young men. Later miners were conscripted bringing the numbers in uniform from this area alone to half-a-million.

Their replacements were men from other industries who could not be expected to be so productive. Then older miners came back into the pits and production was maintained.

Committees were formed to stimulate production; curtailment of statutory holidays was agreed to but any extension of hours was resisted. But voluntary absence was a big problem and Absentee Committees were established at collieries, improving the position a little; real improvement came when the hours of opening of licensed houses was limited.

There were difficulties with supplies because four-fifths of pitprops had come from abroad, from Norway, Sweden and Russia. The War Office allocated a thousand prisoners of war to fell and saw home-grown timber.

The sale of beer was not the principal worry of the Partners at the Brewery for there was a keen demand for all they were allowed to produce. The money position was the problem. W.J.C. asked the Brewery solicitors, Bryan and Armstrong, if a case might be submitted to Counsel to see if mortgages could be reduced BEFORE declaring profits since only he and Edward Titley were ploughing back profits into the Brewery and the Baily interests had stopped doing so.

Since the Bailys had the benefit of their father's estate as to income and not as to capital it is understandable that they wanted some of their eggs in another basket. If Gertrude – Mrs. Thomas – died without leaving children the residue would go to the sons of William Jackson Chadburn as next of kin.

In 1916 the Summer Time Act first came into force on 21st May and later in the year Lloyd George formed his War Cabinet.

The Mansfield Railway was proving a welcome diversion for W. J. Chadburn in the midst of his many problems. The service between Nottingham Victoria and Edwinstowe was opened with great expectations. The first train left Nottingham Victoria at 7.30 a.m. on 2nd April 1917. Despite a heavy snowstorm it arrived at Mansfield at 8.15 and continued on to Edwinstowe and Ollerton.

The Directors enjoyed their celebration journey at a more congenial hour and in a special train that arrived at Ollerton from Nottingham in time for a celebration lunch at the 'Hop Pole Hotel'. The inevitable speeches praised the efforts of the Bolsover Colliery Company and the Duke of Portland and it was later agreed than an annual coal output of three million tons could be expected from the new pits at Blidworth, Farnsfield and Bilsthorpe.

Early in 1917 coal mining came under the authority of the

Board of Trade and a Coal Controller was appointed. (This Government control came to an end on 31st March 1921.)

In the country generally the situation was bad and 1917 was probably the worst year of the war for food and fuel shortages; it also happened to be one of the best years ever for the harvest.

Gertrude and her husband, now a Captain, had moved back to her house, 'The Acre', at Worthing. The main sum they received from the Brewery usually arrived in February, following the audit of the figures to the previous 31st December. At the beginning of 1918 W.J.C. told Gertrude that they were too busy and too short-staffed to carry out the audit but that they hoped to do so early in April. Gertrude, apparently mollified, replied that she would share proportionally again with whatever the Partners decided to plough back.

As the war came to an end Gertrude wrote telling W.J.C. that they were back in Plymouth as her husband was at the Garrison Headquarters. She was unusually affectionate, sending her love to her dear Mr. Chadburn. She might also have sent him the news that she was pregnant but she did not. She was thirty-six years of age and the Captain was somewhat older.

Although the prospects for the Brewery were now so encouraging the results so far had been achieved without the assistance of a qualified brewer. Edward Titley had been a pupil for a time at Strettons of Derby and was regarded as The Brewer at Mansfield. Now he and Mr. Chadburn decided to employ a professional. So far, instinct, tradition and experience had determined the quality of the Mansfield brew, successful enough in a way but due to the interest of science and engineering in beermaking it was at last being recognised as a highly sophisticated process.

W.J.C. was fortunate to hear of an experienced man who was not altogether pleased with his prospects at Marston's in Burton-on-Trent. He was 43-year-old S. C. Deakin and he was destined to establish the quality that ensured the future success of the Mansfield brew.

At 5 a.m. on 11th November 1918 Germany signed the Armistice. Little work was done that day for everywhere people danced in the streets and shouted for joy. Church bells were ringing out their celebration peals when S. C. Deakin made his way through the cheering crowds and came down the hill from the station to the brewery for his first interview with Mr. Chadburn. His first sight of the brewery encouraged him for it was surmounted by the decorative railed parapet with a flagpole that he recognised as the trademark of master brewery architect Stovin Bradford. It was a guarantee to S. C. Deakin that the working environment would be right if he was allowed to create the right system within it.

His first impression of William Jackson Chadburn was of a gruff, self-opinionated, pipe-smoking character, a forbidding man at first, yet to whom S. C. Deakin warmed immediately when he was told that he could have a completely free hand so long as he was considerate to the old employees.

The only stipulation S. C. Deakin made was that his judgement was to be accepted in the buying of all materials. This was granted and he was given complete control of the brewery.

Among the early improvements which S. C. Deakin initiated was the conversion of copper boiling from direct fire to steam. In the short time since their installation the coppers had already become damaged by carelessness and the conversion ensured a long spell of life. (It is possible that No. 1 Copper had been taken out of the old brewery.) Probably on grounds of economy the job was not properly completed as the old fire boxes were left in position and the flues not sealed off so that there was a draught of cold air circulating round the coppers, reducing their efficiency.

Water requirements for the whole plant were provided by a 20 h.p. steam engine and pump of primitive design which thumped and clattered away day and night. Because of the noise the night workers were in the habit of shutting down the engine in favour of the town water supply. There was no alternative source of power in the brewery until what was regarded as a new-fangled electric motor arrived after which it was the steam engine that was the standby, although the electric motor had been acquired for this role.

Despite S. C. Deakin's satisfaction at being appointed Brewer in such a fine brewery building he soon found that the quality of the beer was quite appalling by his standards. This was due to the bad state of repair in which the plant had been allowed to fall and to a pinchpenny approach to the purchase of materials.

S. C. Deakin proceeded cautiously, first of all cleaning up the plant and introducing some measure of biological control in which skill he was ahead of his time. The plant was in such a bad state that, for instance, the 4″ rising main between coppers and fermenting room, had not been dismantled, let alone washed through, for years and the bore was reduced to about 1″ by caked-on sludge. The coolers were scaled up and the running-in mains were filthy. Whilst he was able to make considerable improvements with the resources available and with manpower completely unused to such standards as he imposed, he was to some extent held in check by W. J. Chadburn's lack of ready money. W.J.C. had understandably come to believe that an expensive brewery had been built that would not need any further capital expenditure for years. It came as a shock to him, with his other money problems, to be told that renewals were becoming necessary and that there were improvements to be made in the process.

S. C. Deakin had an ally in Francis Chadburn, however, who had done a spell of science at Sheffield University and who influenced his father in favour of the Brewer's recommendations. Mr. Deakin found that Mr. Chadburn's eldest son was one of the few people with whom he could discuss technical problems and had Francis lived they would undoubtedly have solved many of the Brewery's problems together.

Another change at the end of the war was the move from horse-drawn to mechanised transport. From very early days provision was made for stabling about twenty-five horses in common with all breweries built well before the era of the internal combustion engine.

Mansfield Brewery's ground floor was occupied with stabling – right in the middle of the brewery and a potential source of beer spoilage.

Latterly Claude Chadburn dealt with all matters concerning horses although he did not appear to be very fond of them. The horsemen lived in cottages in the brewery yard facing on to Littleworth. The dung cart took a week to fill and it stood outside the kitchen door of No. 1 cottage; from this cottage yeast, or barm as the locals call it, was sold to bread bakers.

Horses broke down and suffered various ailments with great regularity and their treatment and replacement was in the hands of Claude Chadburn's uncle, Tommy Ludlow, and his horse-coping associates.

From the pungent depths of the dark stables Tommy, who was the local veterinary surgeon, would swig sherry with his cronies and threaten everyone within earshot with castration if they did not attend immediately to his requirements.

The war was over and it was discovered that three quarters of a million men had lost their lives on active service, plus one thousand five hundred civilians.

There was a pronounced swing to the left in the political pendulum and in the 1918 Election the Labour candidate, Carter, was elected for Mansfield.

There was wide popular support for the nationalisation of the mines. The miners themselves were able to occupy their minds with the question of national ownership because their thoughts were diverted by comparative prosperity from the necessity of scratching a living.

The rejoicing and the planning of a country fit for heroes was temporarily interrupted by a major influenza epidemic in the winter following the Armistice.

At the Brewery it seemed that the problems of W. J. Chadburn and Edward Titley were coming to an end for in August 1919 they were able to confirm to Verrall that nothing was owing to the bank. The following year, however, when W.J.C. sent their share of profits amounting to £8,999 to Mrs. Abbott and £8,999 to Mrs. Thomas, he asked them for a £5,000 loan each plus a further £5,000 next year in order to set up a reserve fund. Walter Abbott replied immediately that he would think about it and he agreed that no business should be without a reserve fund. He did point out that if his wife invested in his business, Saxone, she would get 15 per cent tax free.

From The Acre Folks, as Gertrude and Captain Thomas were to become known, there was no response.

By 1920 with the lifting of wartime restrictions on brewing, trade began to expand and Mr. Chadburn agreed to the acquisition of four 50-barrel second-hand open fermentation vessels which S. C. Deakin had found at a closed brewery at Pocklington.

The after-effects of the war continued and there were still shortages of many goods. Even coal was in short supply nationally and in the Mansfield area efforts were made to increase production. The Haworth Shaft was sunk in the early 1920s and also shafts at Clipstone and Thoresby, making Bolsover the third largest colliery in the country. Mansfield was now in the centre of the coalfield.

The Labour Movement continued to grow in influence. The trade boom continued and then, towards the end of the year, slowed down. Unemployment rose, then snowballed and between December 1920 and March 1921 the total of the unemployed doubled; it continued to rise and in June there were over two million unemployed. In the coal, engineering and cotton towns there were more people out of work than in jobs.

During the war the Government had taken control of the railways, mines and other public utilities and early in 1921 it was proposed to hand them back to private ownership. The railways were grouped into four main companies, L.M.S., L.N.E.R., S.R. and G.W.R. Of local interest the Midland became part of the L.M.S. The Great Northern, Great Central and Mansfield Railway became part of the L.N.E.R.

One is inclined to regard the Great Central as one of the smaller railways but just prior to grouping it ranked fifth in tonnage carried, thanks to its proximity to the coal mines and heavy industry, being beaten only by such famous names as the Midland, Great Western, North Western and North Eastern.

The Mansfield Railway proved to be much more than a colliery railway. It was part of a much used connection between Tuxford on the Great Northern line and Kirkby on the Great Central main line. In the summer many special trains took this route from Leicester, Nottingham, Mansfield and district to Skegness, Cleethorpes, Bridlington and Scarborough. There was also steady traffic in steel from Scunthorpe and fish from Grimsby passing south each year.

The coal mines were to be handed back to private ownership on 31st March. On 1st April there was a Lock Out. The miners had lost the strike weapon of threatening to hold up supplies of coal because the market in coal had collapsed. The miners were out until the end of July and they then went back to work having gained nothing.

Everywhere, and in all trades, conditions were depressed and wages were reduced all round.

In 1921 there was a Census that showed the population of England and Wales to be 37,887,000 and of Great Britain to be 42,769,000. Improvements in medical knowledge were improving mortality; the way was found even to overcome the dread tuberculosis, though too late to save Francis Chadburn.

In 1921 Mrs. Thomas and Mrs. Abbott received £8,263 each as their share of profits. In writing to thank W.J.C. Gertrude made no mention of his request for her help in the setting up of a reserve fund, confining herself to the intelligence that her son had influenza.

In July W.J.C. went to Worthing to see the Abbotts and the Thomas's. The Abbotts agreed to provide £5,000 immediately and £5,000 next year. Captain and Mrs. Thomas referred the matter to Verrall who, as usual, did nothing.

July went by, August went by; in early September there was a sale of the licensed premises of the Duke of Portland, a marvellous and unique opportunity to secure some profitable new outlets for the brewery in their area.

The procrastinations of Verrall were almost too much for W.J.C. and he wrote an urgent note appealing for a decision before the Portland sale; then he wrote to Walter Abbott appealing for his help in getting a decision from Verrall.

Abbott succeeded in getting a decision. It was against putting money into the Brewery because Verrall considered that the Government might favour Prohibition and what, he argued, would be the future of the Mansfield Brewery if the country went dry.

Even then W.J.C. did not give up. He wrote a long letter to Mrs. Thomas telling her that a considerable enlargement to the Brewery was taking place at great cost; that he had not been able to buy some of the Duke of Portland's properties owing to lack of money. She passed his letter to Verrall and it stayed on the solicitor's desk while W.J.C. fretted. Three months passed before Mr. Chadburn heard from Gertrude, and then it was only to enquire why she had not received her October instalment cheque.

After 1921 the demand for coal fell although exports regained their pre-war level. 1923 was a peak year for exports which then declined.

The brewery trade remained constant and a gradual programme of rebuilding of public houses was undertaken; it was not so much a planned programme as a course determined by the availability of money.

Also at this time, whether money for new and improved public houses was available or not, the attitude of the local bench, at the Brewster Sessions, was another restrictive factor.

An application for a licence to build or rebuild or transfer was never successful the first time it was submitted nor, very often, the second. The Wesleyans, Methodists, Baptists and Unitarians united in a cause to limit the influence of the public house by any means. They were not wholly successful since during these times the 'Victoria' was rebuilt on the site of the 'White Bear' but set back, the licence arrangement involving the surrender of the licence of the 'Grove Tavern' opposite; the 'Black Bull' in Mansfield Woodhouse was a transfer from the 'Old Black Bull' up the yard off West Gate and close to the house where William Edward Baily once lived; the 'Rufford', Chesterfield Road, was a transfer from a public house of the same name at the corner of Queen Street and Stockwellgate (also of the 'Lawn' off-licence). The new 'Rufford' was built to serve the Bull Farm estate; the 'Eight Bells' in Church Street was a rebuild involving the trading of another licence and the 'Crown and Woolpack' also belongs to this era. All these Mansfield public house rebuilds and transfers were designed by Aubrey Lane who, at the time, had the monopoly of architectural services to the Brewery.

At the top of Leeming Street in Mansfield the old 'Stag and Pheasant' was replaced and faced in dressed stone. Higher up the street a row of shops was sold to pay for the new Brewery in 1910.

The 'Eight Bells' in Church Street, Mansfield, a rebuild similar to the 'Victoria' and the 'Stag and Pheasant'.

9

At the beginning of 1922 Francis Chadburn died leaving a widow and three young children. Francis had married Kate Adams from near Whitby, in 1922. They lived at Ollerton House, and had four children, Betty, Peter, Robin and Kathleen, born the year before in 1921. Peter had died as a very small baby. The death of Francis as we shall see was followed closely by that of his father, and his widow sold the house and left the area and built a new house at Cooden Beach on the cliff edge, frightened by the cause of Francis' death and determined to take her children away from the dust and smoke that she felt had contributed to it. Much later Claude was to write to Robin Chadburn asking if he would have any objection to the Brewery buying Ollerton House and converting it into a public house, which was done in 1961. The loss of his eldest son affected W.J.C. deeply and the problems of the business seemed to bear more heavily upon him than ever. Their efforts at increasing production were bearing fruit and further large extensions to the Brewery were being put in hand. Money, as always, was the problem.

The share of profits to go to the Baily interests for that year amounted to £11,669 to Mrs. Abbott and £11,669 to Mrs. Thomas; receiving such large sums it seemed almost beyond belief that they would refuse to help out by lending back money to the Brewery to assist with immediate financial problems.

Yet W.J.C. knew that it would be a battle again, with all his most eloquent appeals destined to gather dust on Verrall's desk.

It so happened that W.J.C. was not to appeal to Gertrude again and that he had had his last battle with Verrall. William Jackson Chadburn died in May 1922 at the age of seventy-four; with his death the adventurous era of the Mansfield Brewery ended and the period of consolidation began.

The problems that the Brewery had to face following the death of W. J. Chadburn were somewhat lessened by the fact that a postwar boom began, getting into its stride in 1922. The country began to settle down, prices fell and wage rates too; the regulations that had been imposed for the war disappeared with the notable exceptions of Summer Time and the restriction of licensing hours.

The Labour Party were emerging to the permanent detriment – as it turned out – of the Liberals. Ramsay Macdonald came to power in 1922: the working man enjoyed a majority for the first time.

Edward Addison Titley was forty-seven when W. J. Chadburn died and Claude Chadburn was thirty-five. From Worthing they received a letter from Gertrude expressing her concern at the death of Mr. Chadburn and her considerable concern regarding the representation of her interest now that W.J.C. was no more.

The non-working share on the Baily side had always equalled the working Partners' share but W. J. Chadburn's position as Trustee of the Baily estate had given him effective control. Now that he was gone the question of his successor as a Trustee would determine the question of control.

Claude's reply to Gertrude was something of a rebuke. He had only buried his father a few days before, he replied, and that event as she knew followed upon the recent death of his brother. He had had no time for business.

Verrall wrote pressing for a meeting in London.

Edward Titley asked Mrs. Abbott and Mrs. Thomas if they could spare anything from their £11,669 cheques to help with the cost of the extensions to the brewery. Walter Abbott replied that they would help. The Thomas's referred to Verrall who did nothing about that matter being concerned with the appointment of a new trustee.

All the interests concerned were agreeable to Claude Chadburn taking over his father's and his brother's shareholding; as for a successor to the W. J. Chadburn Trusteeship of the Baily Trust the Brewery Partners would have liked Walter Abbott to share this responsibility with Claude. Gertrude's husband, however, had taken a dislike to Abbott who, in turn, described Captain Thomas as an unapproachable beggar, utterly unbusinesslike and impossible to reason with.

Edward Titley tried to persuade Walter Abbott to become a

Joint Trustee but Abbott was afraid that if he did so Captain Thomas would refuse to help the Brewery financially.

Verrall was quick to offer his opinion on a matter that did not concern him and he approved of Claude taking over the shareholding of his father and brother. On the matter that did concern him, the appointment of a trustee of the Baily Trust, Verrall did nothing.

The months went by and Verrall said that he was taking Counsel's opinion. Walter Abbott suggested that the Baily Executorship should revert to the executor of W. J. Chadburn which might well have been so but Claude and Edward Titley were anxious to secure the continued co-operation of the Baily interest whose loans to the Brewery were embarrassingly large.

After five months delay Edward Titley issued an ultimation to Verrall telling him that as he was obviously doing nothing they proposed going ahead without him. Verrall offered no apology. To what matter are you referring, he replied.

Edward Titley appealed to Walter Abbott who confessed that he would never be able to reach agreement or pull together with Thomas. Mrs. Thomas, apparently, was now proposing that the Executorship of her father's estate should be placed in the hands of the Public Trustee; she was concerned to protect her son's income for the future. It was the first hint that all might not be well with the only son of Gertrude and Captain Thomas, the last of that particular Baily line.

Towards the end of the year Counsel's Opinion arrived. It proposed converting the Partnership of the Mansfield Brewery Company into a Private Company with limited liability under the Companies Act, also that the present Partners should be Trustees of the Baily Will. The Public Trustee, apparently, would not accept a trusteeship that involved unlimited liability. Finally, Counsel submitted that Gertrude should not accede to the partners' request to advance more money.

Edward Titley's reaction was to ask Verrall if he had considered the cost of forming a limited company and Verrall replied that he had.

Edward Titley prepared a statement of the position of the business as at 8th December 1922 as follows:

The Company owns, without incumbrances (except as hereinafter specified), in Nottinghamshire and Derbyshire, the following licensed properties:

Fully licensed houses	61
Beer Houses	16
Off Licenses	13
	90

In addition, the Company owns at Alfreton an off beer, wine and spirit shop, house cottage and premises, the property having recently been purchased for £800, and considerable alterations, repairs etc., having been executed. This is a case of removal of a very old existing licence to better and more convenient premises.

The Company owns the Victoria Hall at Mansfield which is let on lease at £225 per annum and there is a bar fully licensed attached to it.

And further the Company have on lease a beer house at Whiteboro, Notts at a rental of £160 per annum.

Certain observations are made at the end of these notes which will, no doubt, have a considerable bearing upon any figure which may be arrived at so far as a valuation of everything is concerned.

In the first instance, all the figures are based upon the Kennedy judgement which was delivered on the 24th July 1906, the award being as follows:-

Beer 14/6d per barrel at 10 years purchase
Wine and Spirits, 2/6d per gallon at 10 years purchase
Rent at 18 years purchase

The current figures of the Company show the following results upon the basis of this judgement:-

Per annum	*Capitalised* £
36,865 Barrels of Beer	267,271
8,090 Gallons Wines and Spirits	10,110
£5,620. 3. 9. rents of Licensed Properties	101,160
	£378,541

Observations

1. The Kennedy judgement allows compensation at a profit of 14/6d per barrel, whereas last year the Company's profit per barrel was 27/9.87d.

2. Wines and Spirits as calculated only show a profit for the past year of £981 but having regard to the scarceness and large price of these goods, this was unavoidable, but the average profit for the past five years is £6,292 annually. It should be noted that in the above given figures for wines and spirits, the capitalisation has only been taken on the £981 profit.

3. There is an annual sale of 5284 barrels of beer to Clubs and private trade which are not taken into account on the above given capitalised figures at all.

4. There are also rents of unlicensed properties amounting to £812. 8. 0. per annum, together with considerable amount of land which is as yet undeveloped, and which at present produces little or no rent, and is not taken into calculation, nor are the unlicensed property rents. There is every possibility that the undeveloped land will be marketable in the very near future. No account is taken of unsold coal.

5. The new Brewery with up to date best modern plant maintained in good order, offices, wine and spirit stores, stables, motor accommodation, bottling stores with expensive plant, beer cellars etc., cannot at a most conservative estimate be put down at probably less than £50,000 a sum which in no way represents the cost alone of the new Brewery and plant.

6. There are maltings for which £2,000 was paid 20 years ago, to say nothing of new machinery which has since been installed, also machinery and tools in another rented malting.

7. The average profit on the maltings for the last five years has been £788.11. 0.
Query: Should not this sum be capitalised to increase the profit per barrel of beer?

8. The net profits last year of the Brewery and the maltings were £50,369. 18. 0. free of tax.

9. Note should be made that no deduction has been made under the Kennedy judgement so far as the properties unlicensed are concerned, but it is strongly felt that having regard to the lowness of the rents and the situation of the properties this matter need in no way be taken into account.

10. Except so far as the Partners are concerned, the total outside indebtedness amounts to £5,050 which sum bears interest at 5%.

11. The Partners capital stood in the last Balance Sheet at £174,675.14. 3.

12. The profit on the sales of cigars and cigarettes is ignored.

13. All the properties both on and off licence are insured against loss on the grounds of misconduct etc., as against the 1904 Act.

14. No account has been taken of Motor Lorries, horses, drays, harness, all casks and other loose tools, the value of which is appreciable.

15. The question of goodwill is not dealt with.

16. This, so far as we are aware, represents the whole case for the Company as now existing.

The properties are all in a fairly good state of repair except that some five premises will shortly have to be reconstructed owing to street improvements being demanded by the Mansfield Corporation, when in four of these cases compensation will have to be paid.

The beginning of the new year of 1923 found Edward Titley and Claude taking Counsel's opinion and Titley wrote to Verrall that there would be Capital Duty on formation amounting to £5,000 plus 1 per cent duty on the value of all licensed houses, the Brewery, maltings, goodwill, assets, probably another £5,000. He hoped that Verrall appreciated the enormous expense to which he was putting Claude and himself.

The Brewery accountants, Mellors Basden of Nottingham, drafted a scheme that gave the Executors of Baily equal voting rights with the Partners.

The Brewery solicitors, Bryan and Armstrong, pointed out that whereas the sleeping Partners' share, plus their loans, gave them a capital interest in the Brewery of considerably more than half, it was upon the resident and working Partners that the success of the Brewery depended. W. J. Chadburn's position as sole trustee of the Baily Trust had, of course, given the working Partners control during his lifetime.

The accountants and solicitors of the Brewery devised a draft scheme, and in January Edward Titley sent it to Verrall. Verrall sent it to his accountant who recorded that he was most impressed by the results of the Mansfield Brewery business and by the nature of the assets, a pleasant sound indeed to come from the Verrall camp whose only opinions of the Brewery so far had been critical.

In May a cheque for £13,440 went to Mrs. Abbott and a similar sum to Gertrude Thomas. Edward Titley expressed the hope that they would use some of it to take up 6 per cent Mortgage Debentures in the new company.

It was agreed that Claude and Captain Thomas should be Trustees of the Baily Trust. It was proposed that Walter

Abbott and Captain Thomas should become directors of the new company along with Edward Titley and Claude. Verrall wrote that Captain Thomas would agree to become a Director but that he had not decided if they would take up any of the new 6 per cent Mortgage Debentures, the difficulty being that the £26,000 Gertrude had lent to the Brewery was included in her Marriage Settlement to the Captain.

Edward Titley and Claude were hoping to receive financial help from the Abbotts and the Thomas's. Instead they heard from Verrall that the £26,000 would have to be paid out under the Marriage Settlement. Edward Titley asked to see a copy of the Marriage Settlement. By June he was appealing to Verrall to hasten approval of the draft scheme he had submitted in January, complaining of the dilatory manner with which affairs were being handled and pointing out that he and Claude had an interest equal to the Bailys.

A month later Edward Titley appealed to Mrs. Thomas to try to persuade Verrall to speed up the business of forming the limited company since the constant delays were making life very difficult for the Partners. As this appeal made no impression Edward Titley wrote to Walter Abbott, confessing that he felt most down-hearted. It was obvious to him, continued Edward Titley, that Gertrude, influenced by Captain Thomas, was in no way disposed to help matters at all at Mansfield. All the work and worry is at the Mansfield end, he complained, and all the Thomas's have to do is to receive large cheques. Edward Titley finished by saying that he had had no holiday since 1914 and he was seriously wondering if the game was worth the candle to be treated in this manner.

Walter Abbott commiserated and assured Edward Titley that he found Thomas to be an impossible individual. Even Verrall had found him difficult for when the solicitor asked his views on putting money into the new Debentures Thomas's only reaction was to fly into a rage.

In addition to the tantrums of Thomas there were always problems to be solved at the Brewery. By 1923 the Brewery was again under capacity and the first extension since 1906, the extension of the Fermenting Room to accept eight more 50-barrel vessels was undertaken, but only two vessels were installed at first.

The British coal industry received help from unexpected quarters in 1923 when the French occupied the Ruhr and there was a coal strike in America. Coal exports felt an immediate and much-needed benefit as did many Mansfield wage packets.

The Brewery trade was obviously dependent upon the prosperity of trade generally although the miner's pint was high on his list of priority spending.

Another factor at about this time that was taking trade from public houses in some parts of the country was the enormous popularity of the cinema but the Mansfield Brew was not noticeably deserted on this account.

A year after he had first submitted the draft scheme to Verrall, Edward Titley wrote to the solicitor asking him whether he was taking any steps whatever to push forward the scheme laid before him for limiting the liability of the Brewery company.

Edward Titley's reminder produced another Counsel's Opinion on the lines that the Brewery must make a Debenture Issue:-

(1) to provide working capital

(2) to pay off £26,000, Mrs. Thomas's Marriage Settlement

(3) to pay off the loans of Mr. and Mrs. Abbott.

The arguments dragged on for another three months. Then Verrall sent the Brewery a bill for the expenses that their side had incurred in consulting Counsel and accountants. Claude sent the bills back saying that they would not consider paying Verrall's clients' expenses, particularly since they were the ones who had asked for a company formation in the first place, and had then hung up the whole business for nearly two years. Verrall tried again and Edward Titley confirmed that the Brewery would not pay these expenses.

In June Walter Abbott decided that he could not join the Mansfield Brewery Board of Directors along with Thomas explaining that it was impossible to get on with such a man.

In September the Mansfield Brewery accountants were able to prepare a preliminary agreement for the formation of The Mansfield Brewery Company Limited with a capital of £350,000. Claude and Edward Addison Titley were to be Joint Managing Directors and Captain F. K. M. Thomas an Ordinary Director.

But the battle had proved too much for Edward Addison Titley and a month before the preliminary agreement was prepared he died at the age of forty-nine.

Once more Harriet was left a widow and still at a compara-

Addison Titley

Edward Addison Titley

tively young age. Her eldest son by her first marriage was now twenty-five and he showed interest in taking advantage of his step-father's shareholding in the Brewery. So Harry Jarvis became a Director of the new Limited Company in place of Edward Addison Titley, joining Claude Chadburn and Captain Thomas on the Board.

10

The collieries in the Mansfield area were so successful that miners were attracted to them from other parts of the country, from South Wales and Derbyshire. In fact, although over the next ten years or so the number of miners in the country was to be reduced by half, in the East Nottinghamshire coalfield a similar reduction did not take place.

The upward trend of prosperity continued over the long term although the slump and unemployment of 1924–25 and the General Strike of 1926 had yet to be overcome.

Miners working in nearby collieries were able to find houses in Mansfield. The Welbeck Colliery had built nearly a thousand houses to the north of Mansfield: the Bolsover Company's Forest Town was well established as a suburb of Mansfield. Elsewhere the coal owners built colliery villages. To the east of Mansfield a new village was built at Blidworth. The Staveley Coal and Iron Company, who were joint owners of Newstead Colliery with the Sheepbridge Company, sank the Blidworth Colliery in 1924. As it turned out it was sunk on a fault and was not worked for some years.

The Butterley Company's New Ollerton Colliery village of nearly a thousand houses was constructed of red brick, and the houses were not built in the usual ranks but in groups surrounded by lawns and gardens. An added novelty to the toilet facilities in each house was the supply of water heated by exhaust steam from the colliery. The Butterley Company also built a factory and rented it to a hosiery manufacturer so that the miners' womenfolk might find convenient employment. Here, too, was a church and an institute, also a clinic and a sports ground.

The coal owners went out of their way to provide satisfactory living and recreational facilities in these instances and the colliery villages of Bolsover and Ollerton were said to be models of their kind.

Having gone all their lives with no facilities provided for them, some of the miners now had colliery village homes equipped with baths, and pithead baths proposed too. The Mining Industry Act of 1920 imposed a Welfare Levy of a penny a ton to provide baths, medical centres, canteens and welfare institutions. The institutions went to the Brewery for their supplies, and the members were well satisfied with the result.

An odd reluctance to use the pithead baths was most noticeable amongst the older miners; they seemed to prefer to wear their grime home with them like a uniform. But they appreciated the sports grounds and the reading rooms that became a feature of many mining villages.

To the brewers competing in the area the miners' institutes presented a challenge and an opportunity. They were not sales outlets that could be bought and then tied like a public house. Successful trading in the miners' institutes depended solely upon the quality of the product and the Mansfield Brew was clearly a firm favourite with the miners.

The installation of the beer in a free outlet was carefully supervised by the brewing staff, who would refuse its entry into any old cellar. There had to be some promise that it would be properly managed and looked after. In particular, standards of cleanliness of the equipment, for raising the beer to the bar counter and into the glass, had to be instilled into those responsible and quite an educational programme embarked upon. It was, and indeed still is, all too easy for poor cellar management to result in good beer being ruined. Foul air drawn into a cask will reduce the life of any beer which must contain CO_2 to give it sparkle. In those days, however, CO_2 was introduced haphazardly by leaving some of the yeast to breathe, and great care was needed not to disturb the ullage in the belly of the barrel or the beer could quickly become undrinkable. Mr. Deakin was not the man to let ignorance ruin his beer if he could help it – in fact he was a very strict disciplinarian whether with employees or, when necessary, with customers, and a potential customer needed his approval before being entrusted with any of the Mansfield Brew.

The miners and other workers were gratified to see the Labour Party in office in 1924, a notable event in political history although, as it happened, Ramsay Macdonald did not last out the year in power on that occasion.

At Mansfield the Limited Company was formed at last on 7th February 1925 and the three families who had principally featured in the creation and development of the Brewery were represented on the Board: the Baily family (who had started it all seventy years before), by Captain Thomas, the Chadburn family and the Titley family, (without whose efforts there would probably have been no business to form into a limited company), by Claude Chadburn and Harry Jarvis respectively.

It was apparent that no practical help could be expected from Thomas and, clearly, he was only tolerated by reason of the Baily shareholding. Harry Jarvis, though willing and friendly, lacked experience, so that from the outset the administrative burden fell on Claude Chadburn, then thirty-eight years of age.

William Jackson Chadburn might be likened to a thrusting buccaneer of a business man, devoted to an idea and determined to achieve his ends even if they seemed to others to involve financial risk. We shall never know how his eldest son Francis might have turned out; he seems not to have taken life quite so seriously as Claude, but then he was never faced with the same problems. Claude set about consolidating what his father had helped to create, and he concentrated on doing his best to see that the Company paid its way and kept out of debt. The Brewery expanded its trade and achieved a stability under his leadership that has paid dividends ever since.

Claude Chadburn may have been criticised in later life for not taking financial risks. For most of his long years in command the standing of the Brewery was so progressively impeccable in the money market that he could have borrowed almost any sum he cared to mention for further expansion. But Claude had witnessed the stresses and strains that borrowed money had imposed upon his father and Edward Addison Titley, and one cannot help noting that William Jackson Chadburn had a number of stress illnesses and died at the age of seventy-four whereas Claude Chadburn has enjoyed an illness-free life.

Claude had been fortunate to qualify in the hard world of 'Paying Money Back'; he had seen the sourness of the insistence on repayment before the sweetness of the temptations to borrow. Cash flow was not a term that had been invented then but the Brewery certainly had it. The shrewd Claude had seen how the bankers constantly pressed for repayment from the Brewery when it was successful and might have wondered what they might do to businesses less fortunate. He may well have resolved early on that no banker or other moneylender was going to persecute him; and during his long years as Chairman his permission was sought to finance many new projects but he never wavered from his cast iron first principle – that no project could be considered unless there was the money in the bank to pay for it.

William Jackson Chadburn ruled for thirty-nine years of adventure, Claude for thirty-six years of consolidation; history has been kind to the Mansfield Brewery in producing the right chairman at the right time.

Of course Claude was fortunate to have S. C. Deakin masterminding the production of the Mansfield Brew which, after all, one might say was the whole business. If Deakin's judgement and skill and integrity was right what other problems could there be now that the panacea of the company formation had covered over former differences and worries? S. C. Deakin produced the golden stream and Claude Chadburn was the right man by temperament and experience to sit in the Counting House.

The coal industry had prospered after the strike and the difficulties of 1921 but in 1924 it ran into trouble with foreign, particularly German, competition and was suddenly in a bad way again. A cut in wages or longer working hours was the answer proposed by the coal owners. Chancellor of the Exchequer Winston Churchill had organised a return to the gold standard and coal was priced out of export markets. In addition, the coal industry had not brought itself up to date or modernised mining techniques in the way that foreign competitors had; there was also competition from oil. The effect of the return to the gold standard on an inefficient industry was disastrous. Wages were reduced to keep export prices competitive. The usual solution to insoluble problems was tried – a Court of Inquiry which, like most such exercises, stated officially what everybody already knew.

A proposed strike of coal miners produced from Prime Minister Stanley Baldwin the announcement that the Government would not help with a subsidy. The T.U.C. threatened a General Strike and the Home Secretary, Sir William Joynson-Hicks, wanted to know if England was to be governed by Parliament and the Cabinet or by a handful of trade union leaders!

The Prime Minister was pressing for wage reductions all round to put industry on its feet. In April 1926 reductions in miners' wages were announced and General Strike notices were prepared but the T.U.C. Printers at the *Daily Mail* refused to print an article that was critical of the unions.

The General Strike started on Tuesday 4th May 1926 and the response to the strike call was almost overwhelming. Yet all were back at work nine days later after a good deal of good humoured strike-breaking; all, that is, except the miners on whose account the struggle had commenced. Even by September not all of the miners were back at work. They were eventually starved into submission, led on by a militant left wing under their uncompromising leader, A. J. Cook, to continue the stoppage for too long. It was a blow to the Miners' Federation that left them in no position to protect their members in the years ahead. After all their suffering the miners went back at lower wages and longer hours than before. So far as the Brewery were concerned the General Strike passed them by, largely because the employees refused to strike in isolation from other breweries in the County.

Claude Chadburn was finding that the Brewery ran quite smoothly without too much intervention on his part. The key to its success was obviously the quality of the beer and this was in the capable and industrious hands of S. C. Deakin. As for the day-to-day running of administrative detail there was Harry Jarvis in the office now; he was obviously not so efficient or experienced as his step-father had been but Edward Addison Titley had provided him with a good example of integrity and business dealing, and he was a trained accountant, having been with Deloittes for some time.

The employees were happy. In those days there were not so many claims upon a man's attention. Hours worked were long and they looked forward with relish to simple pleasures, like the annual outing when the men loaded beer on to an excursion train and had a fine day off at Skegness or Yarmouth, Blackpool or Scarborough, the only time many of them ever saw the seaside.

These outings grew so popular that the womenfolk wanted to come, then outsiders wanted to come, and slowly the atmosphere was changed; but, in any case, when paid holidays began, there was not the same need for an outing.

Claude Chadburn had recently bought Papplewick Hall, an

elegant stone edifice in the Adam style, built in the 1780s. This charming mansion was situated in a peaceful rural setting, enfolded by gentle green slopes and yet almost within sight and sound of the hideous pit-head gear of Hucknall Colliery, a contrast reminiscent of D. H. Lawrence.

Mr. Chadburn was able to insulate himself somewhat by buying part of the adjoining Newstead land which gave him an estate of about 1,400 acres. With Papplewick Hall he became much pre-occupied and during the shooting season enjoyed his sport there and elsewhere three and four times a week. He became one of the outstanding pheasant shots in the district and much in demand throughout the Dukeries where some of the best organised shooting in the country was to be had. His golf too was a by-word and he was a founder member of neighbouring and now famous golf clubs.

He carried on his father's tradition of service to the community – was High Sheriff of the County and was Chairman of the Mansfield Petty Sessional Bench for many years.

At the age of twenty-seven Harry Jarvis suddenly found himself to be the virtual boss of a brewery, quite without the supervision that might have helped him with his particular problem. He was unmarried, a friendly, likeable man who found it difficult to resist the temptations of the drink all around him. He was not called upon to make any major decisions because, since most major decisions were concerned with money, they could only be dealt with by Claude, whose views, in any case, were predictable.

The greatest responsibility was carried by S. C. Deakin and he endured the greatest frustration; but this was eased for him in 1928 when he was joined by his twenty-two-year-old son, Edward, who came in as a pupil in 1926 and had subsequent training elsewhere. Together they ensured the continued excellence of the Mansfield Brew. It was a harmonious father-and-son relationship not often found in business and one whose value to the Brewery over the years it would be impossible to exaggerate.

At this time there was an increasing demand for bottled beer but the Brewery facilities were inadequate to cope with it.

Bottling of naturally conditioned beer was well established by the turn of the century and tentative efforts were being made to produce a sediment-free beer of longer life and greater stability. The answer lay in chilling to throw out the yeast and sediment and in filtering to produce brilliancy, but the necessary machinery was beyond the financial resources of many hundreds of small breweries.

Bottling at Mansfield had started well before 1900 but it required quite a large labour force of women.

It so happened that S. C. Deakin had previously worked at a brewery where the bottling of non-sediment beers had been pioneered. He set about trying to persuade Claude Chadburn to change their methods, and eventually in 1930 secured agreement to install a small two-barrel per hour chilling plant. S. C. Deakin knew that this was completely inadequate but it was all that Claude would permit and, at least, in proving its value, it would provide a satisfactory argument for the installation of a bigger plant.

The small chilling plant was so successful that it created an ever-increasing demand for bottled beer and S. C. Deakin was gratified to have proved his point. But even with the indisputable evidence of the sales figures Claude was mildly sceptical, and it was difficult to persuade him that the successful sales of bottled beer were anything more than a flash in the pan.

The depression years of 1929–1932 slowed down and almost stopped further development at the Brewery for the time being except, perhaps, for the most urgent repair jobs. Britain came off the Gold Standard in 1931 and coal exports improved, but the improvement did not last for very long.

The Nottinghamshire coalfield did better than the rest of the country, although in fact the coal industry was having an unprofitable time. Around Mansfield, perhaps Annesley was the most disappointing of the Leen Valley collieries but the Nottinghamshire mines were generally more successful than others because they were bigger – and they were bigger, of course, because the prospects of coal were better. They were bigger – because the coal measures lay in thicker seams than in other fields and consequently the coal was much easier to get. The Nottinghamshire mines produced considerably more coal than the Derbyshire mines from less than half the number of pits.

In the country generally it seemed that a figure of one and a half million unemployed was an irreducible minimum, for no improvement in this figure had been achieved throughout the 1920s. For the first three years of the 1930s the number of unemployed rose to three million.

Despite this the East Midlands collieries were in a better situation than most, mainly because their success had enabled them to spend money on up-to-date equipment such as the most modern coal cutting machines and mechanical conveyors. Not only was their production superior to the mines of neighbouring Derbyshire but it was well above the national average. Perhaps their thirst was too!

The Brewery was fortunate to have as its principal customers the coal miners and workers in heavy industry whose beer drinking exceeded that of other members of the community, particularly since beer drinking in the country as a whole did not increase in line with the prosperity that came in the late 1930s. Perhaps the recent attraction of talking pictures, or 'talkies', was providing a diversion.

Amidst this increasing prosperity the tram-car, which had enjoyed considerable success until now, began to lose out in favour of buses, although the trolley-bus enjoyed an interim moment of glory. And in 1930 the speed limit of 20 m.p.h. on the roads was abolished.

New smokeless fuels were being developed in the Mansfield area. Coke ovens and tar distilleries were quite common but 'Coalite' was developed by Low Temperature Carbonisation who achieved such success that they needed to open a third plant at Bolsover.

Research was undertaken to assess the possibility of making petrol from coal and a limited success was achieved with Welbeck English Spirit selling for 1s. 2½d. a gallon from petrol stations operated by the Hucknall Collieries.

The Coal Utilisation Council was formed by the coal owners to promote the sale of coal.

The economy of the country began to move in a healthy direction. The number of cars on the roads was increasing to such an extent that it was found necessary to impose a speed limit of 30 m.p.h. in built-up areas and this was put into effect in 1934.

The prestige of the nation was enhanced by the launch of the liner R.M.S. *Queen Mary*. 1,018 feet in length, she had needed three hundred thousand men to build her at a cost of four and a half million pounds.

In the Silver Jubilee Year of King George V, 1935, Claude Chadburn was well established as Chairman of Mansfield Brewery and he had every reason to be satisfied with his business and private life. His future was as secure as it was possible to make it and he had two sons to succeed him in the brewery business when he felt like retiring. It added to his feeling of well-being to be able to offer them such a rewarding future.

It was nearly fourteen years since his elder brother, Francis, had died and Claude could not but reflect that had he lived Francis would have shared the burden and responsibility that he had accepted on his own younger shoulders. With the death in the same year (1922) of both Francis and his father, money was put aside in the form of non-risk capital for the widow and surviving family of three children – Betty, Robin and Kathleen. The Brewery was still a partnership and the complications of becoming a public company were still to be faced at that time. Francis' widow moved with the children to the south coast but died only a few years later in 1929, the children being brought up by a guardian who, having accepted that trust from their mother, gave up her own life to supervise their upbringing under the eyes of Trustees, of whom one was Claude. Some time later when thinking in terms of Robin training for a career, Claude with two sons of his own, could only regret that there were no prospects at Mansfield for Robin. The three boys were at school together at Malvern College at the time.

The Mansfield Brewery proceeded on a comparatively uneventful course, accumulating profits with agreeable regularity. So long as its outlets were provided with a popular beer of consistent and excellent quality there was no reason why success should be denied to the Brewery. Deakin Senior and Junior worked conscientiously to maintain the quality and output, Claude Chadburn was happy with Papplewick Hall, Captain Thomas was happy receiving his wife's share of the profits, but there can be no doubt that the health of Harry Jarvis was beginning to suffer from the generous hospitality that he showed to those with whom he did business, and the entertaining that he felt was expected of him by so many of his friends. He had married in December 1931, and his best man, Brian Bunting, a friend from his accountancy training days with Deloittes, remained a friend and trustee of Harry's wife Sheila all her life. In fact Harry had been Brian's best man in his turn. Sheila did all she could to modify the temptations that Harry was surrounded by, but there was little known medically that could help her, and Harry's attitude of extreme sociability led to a deteriorating situation.

When you look at the contributions made at this time by the respective principals of Mansfield Brewery it might be thought that it would be impossible for an established brewery to fail. Yet obviously Claude had the right touch on the helm and the Brewery proceeded safely on a profitable course through the integrity and persistence of the Head Brewer and his son Edward; and obviously Harry Jarvis kept the administration going.

Harry Jarvis

Frank Munro-Thomas, just before his retirement from the Board.

11

If any proof was needed of the total dependence of a brewery upon its brewer this was furnished in 1934 when the Mansfield Brewery were informed that the Chesterfield Brewery were in a bad way; and after receiving reports from their accountants Mansfield Brewery decided to take over the Chesterfield concern.

The brewery building at Chesterfield was in good condition and money had been spent in an attempt to modernise the equipment, but they had no S. C. Deakin and Son; the quality of the beer was poor. The Chesterfield Brewery, situated at the edge of the Peak District, owned attractive country inns, town hotels and pubs, but of what value are attractive pubs if the beer is unacceptable?

It is quite incomprehensible that owners of fine businesses should watch them die when a remedy is within view for all to see, but companies are not always fortunate in their administrators. With good quality beer the Chesterfield Brewery trade would not have deteriorated; in fact as soon as it received a transfusion of the Mansfield Brew sales made a spectacular recovery.

Chesterfield has been a market town with an interest in metallurgy going back to the Middle Ages, and it expanded rapidly when the coalfields were developed through the coming of the North Midland Railway.

Chesterfield probably became more industrialised and at an earlier date than Mansfield because coal was being mined in that area considerably earlier than in the Mansfield area. This could account for the presence of heavy industry in Chesterfield and this in turn could have led to the development of the three breweries there from early days.

By 1935 the Brampton Brewery was well established and was reasonably well equipped, run by a board of absentee directors but with a professional brewery chairman who was not popular. Scarsdale Brewery was a small family concern owning about thirty public houses in and around Chesterfield. The Chesterfield Brewery was the other business. This had been started by a group of Derbyshire landowners, including the Devonshires and Rutlands on whose vast estates were many public houses which it became convenient to supply from their own brewery. Over the years purchases and leases brought the number of properties to around the hundred mark at which figure the estate stood when Mansfield Brewery became interested.

The original partnership of the Chesterfield Brewery had been formed on 4th July 1853 by a gentleman named Mansfeldt Forster Mills, and others. The company had been constituted by a Deed of Settlement dated 25th March 1884 with a capital of £100,000 in 1,000 shares of £100 each, paid up to the extent of £80 per share and the partners were:-

Mansfeldt Forster Mills	224
Robert William Mills Nesfield	248
Samuel Burkitt	136
William Wynne Jeudwine	136
Robert Fenwick Mills	32
William Burkitt	15
Richard Tesdall Dewé	8
Mansfeldt Henry Mills	1

They faded away and when the last member of the Mills family died – he had lived in style at Tapton Hall during the prosperous days of the Brewery – his nephew, Humble Birkett, returned from Australia to claim his heritage; having endured a life style imposed by his name and his lack of resources he spread himself in splendour at Stubbin Court. The source of his money was of no concern to Humble, only the money itself. He was happy to leave the management of the Brewery to the two Managing Directors, Attrill and Bird.

Attrill managed the commercial side and Bird, a man of considerable charm, the technical. Both preferred play to work. The success of a brewery, as we have seen, can depend in the first instance upon the brewer and clearly the success of the Chesterfield Brewery was in the hands of Bird. Unfortunately for the Brewery he owned trout fishing in Derbyshire and one of

An example of an early scheme to up-date, in this case the 'Pheasant Inn', Mansfield.

the best salmon beats on the Tweed.

The affairs of brewing were therefore left to Charlie Whiting, a devoted assistant who worked long hours to little avail. Whiting up to 1935 lived at the Brewery House where he was on call day and night, and was expected to attend and cash up at T. P. Wood's bars nightly. He was up betimes to mash and start the day's brew. He was a charming and self-effacing man who at the time of the takeover was at pains to indicate that he had no technical training in brewing; but what he lacked in the sciences he more than made up for in knowledge and experience of the trade. His joining the staff at Mansfield smoothed many a rough path in the years of integration, and his help to younger members of the staff was unstinting. What reserves of capital the Chesterfield company had accumulated had been dissipated on palatial licensed premises like the 'Hollingwood', the 'Duckmanton' and the 'White Post', Farnsfield. The 'Hollingwood' had a concert hall, a restaurant and a bowling green, of no appeal whatever to the pub customer of these parts whose first concern was for the quality of the beer.

At one time the big towns, Sheffield and Derby, sent charabanc loads of trippers to the Peak and later the new style trippers in their cars jammed the lanes and delightful peak villages where the Chesterfield Brewery were attractively established . . . if only they had sent out attractive beer to sell. They were in Spitewinter, Birchover, Stanton-in-the-Peak, Ashover, Milltown, Barlow and Troway; at Bakewell and Baslow there was a selection of fine pubs to cater for the thousands of visitors to nearby Chatsworth House.

The acquisition of the Chesterfield Brewery was an exciting development in the history of the Mansfield Brewery, which was soon capable of supplying the increased output needed by the public houses taken over. The Chesterfield Brewery was only doing 100 brls. per week with an estate of nearly one hundred houses; but this called for more fermenting capacity at Littleworth and the voids in the Fermenting Room were filled by new 50 brl. vessels; the old Pocklingtons were replaced also by new 50 brl. vessels.

The brewery buildings at Chesterfield were sold after all the usable plant had been removed.

As soon as the pubs that had been taken over from the Chesterfield Brewery began selling the Mansfield Brew their sales of beer leapt dramatically.

One of the attractions and, to a large extent, an underlying justification for the purchase of the Chesterfield Brewery was that whilst the company leased or owned some 100 properties, in only one or two cases were they contiguous to, and so competing with, Mansfield outlets. The Mansfield Brew was introduced to a large new territory of considerable potential, spread over an area from Ripley up through the old mining areas of Clay Cross and roundabout, and north of Chesterfield to the outskirts of Sheffield, with the Peak houses lying to the west of this industrial belt. Chesterfield beers had never commended themselves to the free trade in these areas but as soon as the Mansfield Brew became established in the new territories, free trade followed very quickly.

Soon the sales exceeded the best ever achieved by Chesterfield beer and went on rising, proving that a much higher level of trade had been possible. When, after only a few years, the trade doubled it became urgently necessary to increase the capacity of the Mansfield Brewery to cope. So during the years 1937–38, and up to the outbreak of war, the rising ground at the back of the brewery was cut away and more accommodation provided for cellarage, cask washing and cask loading. At the same time the company was fortunate in being able to buy an area of land belonging to the Corporation and adjacent to the town electricity undertaking, sufficient to make room for a cooperage, joiners' shop and plumbers' store for the estate department, also a general brewery store.

These problems fully occupied the minds of Claude Chadburn, S. C. and Edward Deakin and, to a lesser extent, Harry Jarvis. James Black Jenkins had been appointed accountant in 1935.

The upheavals in the little world of Mansfield were accompanied by upheavals in the big world outside, the Saar plebiscite in Germany and the election of Stanley Baldwin's Coalition Government in the year that Mansfield Brewery took over the Chesterfield Brewery; next year the death of George V and the Accession of Edward VIII, the commencement of the Civil War in Spain, the Abdication of Edward VIII and the Accession of George VI.

If war was in the air no one realised it and, indeed, how could Claude Chadburn and S. C. Deakin be expected to concern themselves with a faraway political leader called Hitler when their brewery premises at Littleworth were proving quite inadequate to cope with the exciting new production demands that had been unleashed upon them by the acquisition of the Chesterfield Brewery?

A number of processes were still carrying on in the original part of the brewery buildings dating from 1854.

Following the take over of the Chesterfield Brewery the first steps were taken to move processes out of the 1854 Brewery premises and to clear old buildings for further development. As noted earlier, the first and most urgent necessity was the provision of more cellar space and cask washing facilities together with a loading out bank. Unfortunately, on grounds of economy, the cellars were reduced from their original planned area although it was obvious that the available ground could never be reclaimed once the boundary wall was built. The loading bank was, at the same time, adequate to house the nine vehicles which at that time accounted for the full fleet.

The malt, sugar and hop stores were formed out of part of the 1854 buildings. The shell was retained but the new floors were carried on a steel frame built inside this shell. The square of land bought from the Electricity Department was utilised for the cooperage and stores. Work proceeded with the erection and equipping of the first half of No. 2 Fermenting Room. These alterations represented the first phase of a coherent plan for modernising and increasing the capacity of the plant.

In addition to the reconstruction and redesigning of part of the brewery there was progress being made to public houses and to the immediate pre-World War Two era belong the 'White Swan' at Pleasley (taking in the 'Old Spot'), the 'Devonshire' at Sutton, the 'Sir John Cockle' on Sutton Road and the 'Oak Tree' on Southwell Road. Licences transferred to these new sites included those of the 'Star' on Commercial Street, the 'Cross Keys', West Gate and the 'King and Miller', Stockwellgate.

It is interesting to note that when the dust had settled and the Chesterfield Brewery with its public houses had been fully integrated, there were still the old divisions carried forward in men's minds. The public houses of the old Mansfield Estate and around Mansfield, of Sutton-in-Ashfield, Kirkby, Ollerton and Mansfield Woodhouse were still thought of as Mansfield Brewery while the Chesterfield houses were considered as those on the estate over Grassmoor, right down to Ripley, Chesterfield, Bakewell, Baslow and so on. Trade at such places as Sheffield was thought of as new.

Apart from supplying from the brewery at Mansfield the new trade of the hundred or so pubs of the Chesterfield Brewery (a trade that expanded beyond the wildest expectations largely on account of the charm of the Mansfield Brew), there was increasing trade all round. The economy of the country had been recovering steadily and in 1937 the lowest unemployment figures for three or four years were recorded.

Employment figures at the Mansfield Brewery were not dramatically affected by the take-over of the Chesterfield concern. All Chesterfield employees who wished to come to Mansfield were given the opportunity of doing so, but although quite a number availed themselves of this opportunity not many stayed. Jobs were easy to get, and wives yearned to be back where their roots lay . . . and their mothers lived!

In the Mansfield Brewery office the take-over was handled by a small staff: W. T. Gilbert as Secretary and John Hardy, Senior Clerk. They were assisted by five clerks and there were no female office employees, not even a telephone girl since the telephone was answered by anyone who happened to be passing.

Most important of all, the quality and production of the beautiful Mansfield Brew was looked after by S. C. Deakin and his son, Edward; they also operated a comprehensive system of public house cellar inspection.

It seemed that there was always some new industrial development that would add more customers for the Mansfield Brew. The Butterley Company's biggest venture in the Mansfield area, at Ollerton, became fully operational in 1937, having taken six years to sink and ten years to prepare.

Newspapers everywhere were full of the affair of the Duke of Windsor and Mrs. Simpson. The soon-to-be-familiar Air Raid Precautions were introduced which, at least, showed an awareness of the possibilities in store despite the countrywide belief that, somehow, peace would be maintained.

Europe prepared for war but all other problems were driven from Claude Chadburn's mind at the end of 1938; after a happy Christmas with the family at Papplewick, his two sons, John Ludlow Chadburn (Ludlow being Claude's mother's maiden name), and Alan William Chadburn went out for a drive in Alan's sports car. Near the gates of Newstead Abbey Alan pulled out to overtake a slow-moving lorry and as he did so the lorry turned into his path. A collision was unavoidable. Alan was taken to Mansfield Hospital but his brother had received fatal injuries. John was eighteen years of age.

Hitler annexed Austria and during the Munich crisis civilian gas masks were issued in Britain. The Spanish Civil War ended and World War Two began. Germany had invaded Czechoslovakia and then Poland. Britain was at war and National Service (Conscription), was introduced.

The war prevented the completion of further plans to improve the productive capacity of the Brewery but the opportunity arose in 1944 to buy five acres of land on Great Central Road to house the bottling stores when they could be cleared from a section of the 1854 building. Another square of land was bought and earmarked for the erection of a new boiler house.

Also in 1947 the Labour Government eased the granting of building licences and the chance was seized of extending No. 2 Fermenting Room and partly equipping it. Then building restrictions were very quickly imposed again. After long and protracted negotiations with the Ministry of Food & Agriculture, embodied in the person of a superannuated Brigadier, but with wholehearted co-operation from departmental officers of the local Council, permission was obtained for the removal of the bottling stores.

In the year that war was declared the last remaining five brewery horses had been sold and the area of old stabling was reclaimed for more efficient and hygienic use.

Alterations were completed to the 'Unicorn' at Gunthorpe at a cost of £6,175 (purchased from the Wilson family in 1937. The premises included a maltings at the rear of the public house) and the 'Live and Let Live' at Morton was leased at an annual rent of £104.

The Brewery was about to face a compulsory curtailment of activities and shortages of many kinds; also restriction of dividends.

Just prior to the war there was a surplus of labour in the mining industry but it was thought that many men would be needed to meet the increased export demand for coal, to France particularly. Then, in 1940, France was over-run by Germany and occupied and the coal industry in Britain had too much coal and too many miners. For two years they were allowed to join the Forces and were conscripted.

Divisional Coal Offices controlled stocks and the movement

of coal, often complicated by the bombing of railways, and there was some Government control of the industry.

Millions of children were evacuated during the war from industrialised areas. Milk was provided cheaply for young children and expectant mothers from 1940; then cod-liver oil and orange juice were provided free.

As the war continued a shortage of coal occurred and a shortage of miners. The Mines Department of the Home Office was replaced by the Ministry of Fuel and Power under Gwilym Lloyd George. Ex-miners in the Forces were allowed to leave and return to the mines. Men being called up were allowed to choose work in the mines instead of War Service. The 'Bevin Boy' scheme was introduced under which all boys due to be called up entered a ballot which determined who went into the mines.

Throughout the war there was a very high absentee rate in coal mining which was accounted for by malnutrition and war weariness. To cope with the malnutrition canteens were opened but there was a shortage of beer, said to induce a mild neurosis in men accustomed to drinking large quantities. Public houses opened for as many hours as their ration permitted and men took time off to go in search of beer, and cigarettes too, often following the Brewery lorries round on their delivery runs.

Wages were high everywhere (except in the Forces, needless to say), and miners received a big increase in wages that levelled them up with other workers. The coal owners could well afford it now, particularly those in the Mansfield area. The Staveley–Sheepbridge Group had a bigger production of coal than any other colliery group in the country.

Mansfield Brewery employees, home on leave from the Forces, would find it hard to be denied a pint of their very own Brew; when pubs failed them they would sometimes seek a little at the Brewery but the shortage was so acute that it was not always possible to indulge them as they deserved.

Although the war was turning against us no one so much as considered defeat. Although France had been subdued and the German hordes had invaded Denmark and Norway, the Netherlands, Belgium and Luxembourg we had Winston Churchill in command. We evacuated Dunkirk, endured the blitz and the blackout, surrendered Singapore, evacuated Burma; in the third week of June 1942 we reached our lowest point when we surrendered Tobruk and twenty-five thousand men were taken prisoner.

Tobruk merits more than a passing reference in this history because the remaining son of Claude Chadburn was involved there.

Between the summer of 1941 and the summer of 1942 the battle in the Libyan desert swung to and fro between Mersa Brega in the west and Buq Buq, four hundred miles away in the east.

Tobruk was of key importance because it was the only sheltered harbour between Benghazi and Alexandria. It was of great strategic importance in the defence of Malta and the command of the passage of the Mediterranean. It had been the main military base of the Italians until captured by the Australians in January 1941. Shortly afterwards Rommel and his Panzers arrived in Cyrenaica but only to prevent the Allies from gaining control of the southern shore of the Mediterranean.

After Rommel's initial success Churchill removed General Wavell and replaced him with General Auchinleck, Commander-in-Chief, India. After many battles and losses on both sides of men and materials the tactical superiority of Rommel was established.

The battle for Tobruk began in early June 1942 and there is an account in the Royal Artillery Commemoration Book of 'The Stand of the South Notts Hussars' (who were officially 107 R.H.A. providing gunner support for the 22nd Armoured Brigade). The following is an extract:

> 'All that night of June 4/5th the men stood to. At 2 a.m. they fired a concentration towards where the enemy were thought to be. As dawn broke the brigade topped the lip of the Cauldron and were received with heavy and accurate fire. The shelling ceased and as the sun rose our tanks poured through the guns and joined battle with the German tanks to the west. From a commanding position on the escarpment Captains Barber and Chadburn of 426 Battery, on OP duty in their Honey tanks could see down into the Cauldron. Tremendous execution was done until the H.L.I. were counter-attacked and forced to withdraw. Captain Barber's Honey had a track blown off and had to be towed out by Captain Chadburn's.
>
> 'About midday the tanks broke off to refuel, bringing with them the tattered remains of the H.L.I. The enemy shelling went on all day. Towards evening a reinforcement battalion arrived. The Group were told that they were to stand and to fight to the last man

and the last round; armoured help would return for them at first light on the 6th. They were not to know that this armoured help would have to be diverted elsewhere.

'As darkness approached fighting intensified, then the night passed quietly with spasmodic shelling. At dawn the shelling started once more. More and more German tanks appeared. Never for a moment did the shelling stop. Casualties became heavier and heavier. Vehicles were burning everywhere and ammunition was running short. Soon German tanks had overrun the infantry battalion in the rear.

'In the afternoon the Germans were attacking to the right. Of the anti-tank guns only one now remained but there was no one to fire it. As evening approached the German tanks were moving in. The Indian Infantry Brigade was completely overrun – there was nothing left of them. Still the South Notts Hussars held out and kept the tanks at bay. Guns were firing in every direction.

'The gallant fight of 425th Battery ended with all killed or wounded.

'Down in the hollow Alan Chadburn's guns were still intact but on all sides the German tanks were closing in, machine guns blazing. The end was very near now. 426th Battery Command Post fell to the advancing tanks; and though in a last defiant gesture Captain Chadburn's F Troop scored two direct hits at eight hundred yards they could do no more.

'Soon that deep silence that descends on a battlefield when the contest is ended spread over the Cauldron.'

Rommel went on, as is well known, to receive the surrender of Tobruk.

The Chairman of the Mansfield Brewery received a telegram at Papplewick Hall regretting that Captain Alan Chadburn had been killed in action on 6th June 1942, sitting on his vehicle firing a tommy gun at the enemy.

12

Eighth Army broke through against the Afrika Korps at Alamein in October 1942 and from then we started to climb. We captured Tripoli, secured the German surrender in Tunisia, invaded Sicily, landed in Italy and secured surrender, invaded Normandy.

On 1st November 1944 the Home Guard stood down. Edward Deakin handed in his rifle but kept his greatcoat and boots, and a host of memories.

Next year, following atomic bombing of Hiroshima and Nagasaki the Japanese surrendered and the Second World War was over. Of greatest relevance to the history of the Mansfield Brewery the war had claimed Alan Chadburn and Edward Titley. Younger half-brother of Managing Director Harry Jarvis, Edward Titley was killed in action while serving as an R.A.F. Pilot.

The Brewery was more fortunate in the Second World War than it had been in the First World War in that its casualties were lighter by far.

In addition to these personal tragedies there had been a succession of problems throughout the war at the Brewery, made no easier by the realisation that every business had suffered considerable hardship. At least the Brewery had been spared bombing and the many licensed houses had also escaped.

Only two fire bombs fell on Mansfield during the war and apart from this there was no war damage at all. The air raid sirens wailed frequently, however, as the German bombers passed over on their way to Sheffield and Merseyside.

The last public house building that the Brewery had managed to get completed was the 'Oak Tree' in Mansfield, built in 1940 at a cost of £7,992, and also the completion of alterations to the 'Queens', Whittington, at a cost of £1,200. No other building was possible and there were no property developments

Then and now. The gardener's cottage at the bottom of Gilcroft House garden, opposite the Brewery . . . now completely urbanised.

except for the leasing of the off-licence in Derby Road, Chesterfield for £100 per annum in 1943 and the purchase of the Hollis Trust Houses for £31,000 in 1944, leased to Chesterfield Brewery.

During the war nett earnings were ploughed back into the company because no capital expenditure was possible and with the restriction of dividends as well it meant that substantial sums of profits were built up and included in reserves.

The years of enterprise and consolidation had built up the value of the Brewery to an impressive figure; and with no effort upon their part the holding of the Baily family had snowballed too. This holding was equal to a half-share, probably a little more, of the Mansfield Brewery and, as we have seen, had come into the hands of Gertrude and her husband Captain Munro-Thomas. The appointment of Munro-Thomas as a token director had been made in the hope and expectation that he would not rock the Brewery's financial boat; and over the years he had honoured this understanding if, indeed, he was aware of it.

The considerable wealth of the Baily holding would normally have passed to the only son of Gertrude and the Captain. The story of the boy, Frank, was the final tragedy of Gertrude's life.

It has been seen how, as a child, she had been moved around like so much of the baggage of her eccentric father; and then as a confidant, companion and witness to the tantrums of her mother, then earning for herself the attentions of a man who turned out to be overbearing and ignorant. But at least, unexpectedly, he gave her a son; she was blessed with woman's crowning fulfilment, the chance to bear another life, for her a wonderful expiation of all her past miseries and denials of love.

It was, in fact, the final blow for she was to endure the agony of watching with mounting doubt and horror the growing up of her only son . . . to the time when he was certified as a lunatic. No wonder that Gertrude died at a comparatively early age, probably of a broken heart.

The son, Frank Baily Thomas, having been born in the second year of the First World War, had come of age and inherited his fortune in October 1937. A trust had been set up for him by Gertrude, the property comprised in the trust being mainly the holdings in the Mansfield Brewery.

As the young man was not capable of dealing with his own affairs it was necessary to apply to the Management and Administration Department of the Court (now the Court of Protection), for the appointment of a Receiver.

The first Receiver appointed by the Court was Frank's father, Captain Munro-Thomas, who set about the business of antagonising everybody in his customary manner. If he had been difficult before the tragic experiences with his son the Captain was now quite impossible; and yet, pathetically, Munro-Thomas tried at length to engage in conversation with his son, seeking to reach some understanding. He made not the slightest effort to reach any sort of understanding with anyone else, however, and quarrelled repeatedly with the solicitors and with the Court over his Receivership of the Baily Thomas Trust. After only a few months any sort of dialogue became impossible and the Captain relinquished his duties as Receiver, having impressed the Court with his incompetence.

Although he was a Director the contacts made by Munro-Thomas with the Brewery were of the briefest nature. He appeared only for the quarterly board meetings, and not always then. For his short stay in Mansfield on these occasions his prickly presence was endured by Claude Chadburn and his wife at Papplewick Hall.

It was apparent that an efficient Receiver of the Baily Thomas Trust needed to be appointed in the place of the Captain and an independent accountant of repute was named; the firm of Chartered Accountants involved was Barton, Mayhew and the partner who finally took on the job was Mr. J. F. T. Nangle.

The Receiver's charge was established in a large country house near Horsham which had been bought when Frank Baily Thomas came into his inheritance in 1937. The household consisted of the son, Frank, his father, Captain Munro-Thomas, and Miss M. E. White, a close friend of Frank's mother who acted as his guardian.

Finding himself as Receiver of a Trust that happened to be composed of half of a prosperous brewery (in fact the Baily Thomas Trust owned 51 per cent), Mr. Nangle naturally took a professional interest in the Mansfield Brewery accounts from then on.

When, in 1941, the Baily Thomas household at Horsham found it impossible to live with the quarrelsome Munro-Thomas it was Chartered Accountant Nangle who had the unpleasant task of asking the Captain to leave. The establishment then continued under the general management of Miss White until her death in 1952 when two members of the domestic staff, Mr. and Mrs. Binstead, undertook to look after Frank Baily Thomas. The Horsham property was sold and a house was bought at Worthing (where today Frank Baily Thomas is still looked after by the Binsteads with great devotion).

Building restrictions continued after the war and the only concession that could be obtained was to house the new bottling machinery in the shed in the old brewery yard, which now forms part of the cellars. This new machinery was urgently required.

After the Germans surrendered in May 1945 Winston Churchill announced that there would be a General Election on 5th July to give the people a chance to choose their peacetime leaders. It was widely expected that Churchill, the wartime leader, would win just as the First World War leader, Lloyd George, had won the 1918 Election.

Surprisingly the people decided that although they valued Churchill for war they did not want him for peace. And so it was Clement Attlee who reported to the startled King George VI at Buckingham Palace and the first Labour Government to be elected with a clear majority was in power.

There were five million bombed homes to be replaced, factories, harbours, railways to be rebuilt, Lease-Lend to be repaid and debts to many other foreign countries that had been incurred during the war. The only way out was to increase exports but what hope was there of this when so many factories were out of action.

The immediate problem was solved by an American loan. The Marshall Aid was signed on 5th June 1947 and the British standard of living was saved for the time being.

Despite economic difficulties the Attlee Government was determined to go ahead with its plans for nationalisation starting, three months after taking office, with the Bank of England. In the first two years of the Attlee Government coal, electricity, gas, transport and civil aviation were nationalised with the laudable ambition to use the profits thus secured to alleviate the burden of the tax-payer and to provide social services. Alas for such ambitions; time was soon to show that nationalisation would increase the tax-payer's financial burden considerably. Strikes and conflicts continued and efficiency deteriorated.

Aneurin Bevan was appointed Minister of Health in 1945 to

The Deakins, father and son

introduce the National Health Service.

The Miners' Federation of Great Britain and the Labour Party had, of course, been committed to a policy of nationalisation of the mines. The National Union of Mineworkers came into being on 1st January 1945.

Although times were difficult for most industries because their basic materials and production were in competition with plans for recovery, the Brewery was under a lesser liability. The working man's wife might be denied pots and pans and clothes but the working man would not be denied his pint. Families could be short of meat and milk, bread, fats and sugar but the miner had to have his beer.

These problems at home moved towards solutions in an atmosphere of comparative goodwill; in world affairs a chill was descending on the comradeships that had been established during the war. Speaking at Fulton, Missouri, Winston Churchill said that from Stettin in the Baltic to Trieste in the Adriatic an iron curtain has descended across the continent.

On 1st January 1947 ownership of U.K. coal mines passed to the State and the blue flag of the National Coal Board flew proudly at pit-heads throughout the country. At some collieries bands were playing on the great day. It goes without saying that the celebrations benefited the brewery trade.

In February 1947 what became known as the Great Freeze-Up began. Coal mines, factories and shops were closed and a great deal of public transport was unable to move. Snowstorms continued, power stations had priority in the supply of coal, the enforced economy of electricity produced blackouts reminiscent of the war.

Once the country had recovered from this particular problem imposed by the weather it was expected that the National Coal Board would ensure peace and prosperity in the mines. It was hoped and assumed that strikes would be a thing of the past, that the 'Them and Us' conflict between coal miner and coal owner had ended with the ownership of the mines by the nation, in part by the miners themselves. But less than five months after nationalisation there was a coal strike and it began to look as though the Coal Board had simply taken the place of the coal owners without much improvement in relationship.

With the first signs of Spring the brewery was looking forward to the Summer trade but it was an expectation tempered with a little sadness because the hand that had guided the Mansfield Brew for almost thirty years withdrew for a rest. S. C. Deakin retired from an executive position with the Brewery on 31st March, 1947 having joined William Jackson Chadburn as the victory bells rang out in November 1918. The obvious is often overlooked but what S. C. Deakin made out of the unpromising brewing conditions he found was the Mansfield Brew; and the Mansfield Brew was, of course, the success of the Brewery.

When S. C. Deakin retired from the day-to-day supervision of the Brewery he remained a Director and Consultant, and whenever Edward brought him down to the Brewery he was welcomed by the men, some of whom had no doubt thought that his retirement would bring to an end his very strict reign. He had been a man with very high standards and without much time for wasters or slackers and he was always treated with great respect. As it happened, Edward was well suited by character and temperament to carry on where his father had left off, and he immediately set about extending the official procedures established by his father. There was still to be no time wasted by those whose employment became his responsibility, although merit and application were seen to be rewarded and everybody knew that they would get a square deal.

Nationalisation continued with the railways on 1st January 1948. On 5th July the National Health Service started and the Gas Industry was nationalised the following May.

The National Health Service was widely welcomed providing, as it did, complete welfare from birth – from six months before birth in fact – to death and with education, sickness, unemployment, medical attention and retirement all provided for 4s. 11d. a week. Everybody had a family doctor for the first time.

In 1948 food rationing still continued and two pints of milk and two loaves of bread were all that were allowed a person for a week. The meat ration was limited to what 1s. 6d. would buy.

The plan at the Brewery that had been devised before the war to re-arrange and reconstruct to improve production had, of course, been held up by hostilities although it had been just possible to put into effect Phase One of the plan between the acquisition of the Chesterfield Brewery and the commencement of the war.

What is known as the hot side of the Brewery had become

overloaded but during the war the only extension that could be made was the deepening of two mash tuns. As soon as it was practicable to do so after the war the boiler house was removed to the new site in 1950, releasing that area for an extension to the hot side in correct relation to the existing plant and precisely coordinated with it.

The boiler house was re-sited as originally planned more than ten years before and in a position suitable for the future requirements of the Brewery. The capacity of the hot side was doubled by the installation of an additional mash tun and all ancillary services, all capable of flexible and integrated working.

At this time space was earmarked for further sugar storage and for a further 180 brl. copper.

By 1949 British exports were rising at last but not by enough to solve our problems. In September the pound was devalued by Chancellor Stafford Cripps.

The meat ration went down to eightpennyworth per person per week but, at least, clothes rationing ended. The newspapers published a front page picture of President of the Board of Trade Harold Wilson symbolically tearing up a book of clothing coupons.

The next phase of the Brewery reorganisation plan was the removal of bottling to the new site and the release of further ground floor space for eventual extension of the fermenting capacity, cask storage etc. The old buildings, formerly bottling stores, were earmarked for a site for hop storage one day, but this project was never carried out.

In 1950 steel was nationalised after much argument and threats by the Conservatives to denationalise steel as soon as they were returned to power.

In January 1950 milk rationing ended but eggs were rationed until August.

The Korean War was having a profound effect on the British economy in that it had influenced the start of a big rearmament programme which naturally diverted productive capacity and materials from much-needed consumer goods. The word 'inflation' began to be heard. National Service, requiring young men to serve for two years in the Armed Forces, was introduced.

In 1951 Harry Jarvis died at the age of 51. It would be useless to deny that his liking for people and his habit of drinking with them had not contributed to his early death. He had been a popular figure, shortish with spectacles that appeared rather prominent, and a waistline that had suffered a bit as the years went by. He had been very keen to help the Brewery employees to find a field to start an inter-Brewery cricket league, unfortunately without success.

A cricket bat was found in a brewery store room and he was asked if the embryo cricket team might have it; with some emotion Harry Jarvis explained that the bat had belonged to his half-brother, Edward Titley, and was therefore of great sentimental value. Because of this he could not let them have the bat but he promised to set them up with a complete set of new gear and did so.

Harry Jarvis had come into a managerial position at the Brewery unexpectedly following the death of his step-father, Edward Addison Titley at the age of forty-nine. And Edward Addison Titley had come into a managerial position unexpectedly following the retirement of his father, Addison Titley, at the age of thirty-seven. With the death of Harry Jarvis, therefore, the Mansfield Brewery ended a connection with the Titley family that had begun in 1873.

For Claude the finish of the Brewery's connection with the Titleys was a considerable milestone. The Baily connection must end, so far as a personal connection was concerned, with the death of Munro-Thomas, since the only son of Gertrude and the Captain, now thirty-one years old, was tragically incapable of handling his own affairs. He, Claude, was sixty-four and the large photograph by his fireplace of the handsome and intelligent young Army Officer was a sad and permanent reminder that he had no son now to follow him in the business, and it began to look as if the Chadburn name would be the next to go.

So far as the efficient running of the brewery was concerned Claude had no particular problem. Success depended upon the quality and quantity of the Mansfield Brew and this was never in doubt.

The Brewery Sports Club that Harry Jarvis had wanted to establish was not forgotten after his death. Edward Deakin continued the search for a suitable ground and finally found one at New Houghton in 1952.

A cricket team was enthusiastically supported by the employees thanks to the encouragement and help given by the

Head Brewer who allowed the use of a van for transport. Edward Deakin and his wife also interested themselves in the provision of food and drink and the regular sporting events would have been empty affairs but for the knowledge that Mr. Deakin would be present with his carving knife and his bustling good cheer.

Mansfield Brewery Cricket Club had a hand in starting a Brewery Cricket League and enjoyed regular fixtures with the teams of other breweries in the area. At the end of each season the breweries would take it in turns to entertain league members to supper; when it was the turn of the Mansfield Brewery to act as hosts they sometimes used the 'Dukeries Hotel' at Edwinstowe.

Football and other sports were catered for also; there was a tennis court, putting greens, tug-of-war teams and everything was gladly provided by the company.

But as the generation who had started the Sports Club grew older, enthusiasm waned; the younger members belonged to a generation who had grown up to watch rather than participate and the club was closed and the ground sold in the late 1960s.

On 6th February 1952 newspapers appeared with black borders. The popular King George VI had died and the young Queen returned from Kenya, having broken her Commonwealth tour.

With the end of the Korean War the world shortage of materials eased and the British economy began to recover. The Conservatives denationalised the steel industry as they had threatened to do. They did not attempt to deal similarly with the other industries that the Attlee Government had nationalised.

The Coronation of Queen Elizabeth II was seen as a happy omen for the future peace and prosperity of the country. At the Brewery the fall in the cost of raw materials was welcomed and, in addition, trade continued to increase, producing a surplus for the year of £90,003. Inevitably the increase in trade produced a bottleneck in production, on this occasion in the fermenting space.

In 1953 a start was made to improve the technical control of fermentation and, at the same time, to increase the fermenting capacity.

Substantial reserves had been built up following the wartime accumulations and it was decided that an issue should be made of one new fully paid Ordinary Share for each share already held, the new issue being rendered fully paid up by capitalising the balance at the credit of the Excess Profits Tax Post War Refund, £5,045, transferring to capital £215,000 from the general reserve and utilising £31,958 from the balance at the credit of the Profit and Loss Account. Nominal capital was increased from £650,000 to £1,000,000. Assets were shown as £586,808 and liabilities £282,961. In this year (1954), additional plant and machinery was installed and the cost of improvements to licensed premises amounted to £17,205.

The splendid surplus for the year was a reflection of the healthier state of the economy. Food rationing ended and at last it was possible to buy enough meat, too much perhaps for, oddly, from the end of rationing the health of the nation slowly deteriorated. In the shop windows were gleaming displays of washing machines, television sets, refrigerators; glittering symbols of the affluent society were to be seen in every High Street.

The Brewery carried out another modest take-over in 1955. A local soft-drinks manufacturer named Hornby had built up quite a prosperous bottling and wholesaling business and, in the process, acquired a number of on and off licences. William Hornby was a hard-working man who could be seen every morning checking his lorry loads in Midworth Street until shortly before his death. He had started from nothing and was particularly proud of having built a number of public houses without any assistance from the bank.

When he died the business deteriorated and the Mansfield Brewery acquired it for cash and shares.

The premises that came to the brewery in this deal were the 'Vine' at Chapel St. Leonards, a holiday pub-type hotel built just before the war and which the Mansfield Brewery eventually sold; the 'Ravensdale' on the Ravensdale estate, a large pub with ample space for development that the trade there did not justify; the 'Savages Vaults' in West Gate that was later sold to the adjoining British Home Stores; the 'Crown' at Southwell that needed extensive modernisation which was carried out; one or two country licences and an off licence; the 'Plough' at Farnsfield which was doing a good trade despite the dilapidated condition of its furnishings and of the property too (contradicting the impression that pubs must be modernised to do well); and the 'Great Northern' at Stretton, an old railway pub dating back to the days of railway excursions.

The soft-drinks manufacture and bottling were transferred to the Littleworth Brewery and the Hornby site was then used by the Mansfield Brewery Estates Department.

It was the purchase of the Hornby business that really sparked off some very big changes in management at the Brewery. Part of the price paid, on professional advice received by Claude Chadburn, was made up of shares issued to the Hornby family. From the time that Claude took the Chair the Company's Accountants had been Mellors Basden & Mellors of Nottingham, and Frank Pragnell, a contemporary of Claude had rightly come to be his friend and adviser. They played golf together and both J. B. Jenkins and F. A. Gleadell came to the Brewery from Frank Pragnell's office, and were to play important roles in its development. It must be assumed that the critical shareholding position was not appreciated when recommendations regarding the purchase of Hornbys and Scarsdale were made. The Hornby move was made while Capt. Munro-Thomas was still a member of the Board, but by that time he had given up the responsibility for looking after the fortune held in trust for his unfortunate son. The Baily Holding in the Brewery was thereby reduced from one of just over 50 per cent to one of slightly less, and unfortunately the first the Receiver responsible to the Master of Lunacy knew of this was on reading through the Annual Accounts for 1957. The Receiver J. F. T. (Jock) Nangle, Senior Partner in Barton Mayhew, the London Accountants, sought permission to seek a seat on the Brewery Board, and clearly there was no denying such a request. Apprehensive of possible trouble, Claude approached Francis' son, Robin Chadburn, who was married with three children, farming in Lincolnshire, an Alderman on the Kesteven County Council and a Partner and Agricultural Adviser to a firm of Architects. There was to be no commitment on either side regarding the future, but an additional family Director was felt to be required to balance the Court's representative. Thus it was that Mr. Nangle and Mr. Robin Chadburn met for the first time at their first Board Meeting on 10th September 1957. As it happened, this was a lively meeting because the purchase of the Scarsdale Brewery in Chesterfield was on the Agenda and one of the possible ways of paying for it was a rights issue – not likely to be unquestionably acceptable to the major shareholders. In the event it was decided not to purchase, and as it happened Robin Chadburn and Jock Nangle found themselves at one on this issue and started a friendship that contributed a great deal to the Brewery in the next 20 years.

On the political scene at this time Churchill resigned in favour of Anthony Eden as Prime Minister and Attlee retired in favour of Gaitskell as Leader of the Opposition.

The early affluence of the emerging society was snowballing too quickly and a credit squeeze was applied to control the seemingly inevitable inflation.

On New Year's Day 1956 the last train ran from Nottingham Victoria Station to Mansfield, Edwinstowe and Ollerton, thus ending a dream of one of the founders of the Mansfield Railway, William Jackson Chadburn. Everywhere, of course, local railway services were being discontinued in the face of competition from the motor-car. The use of the car was somewhat restricted in this year, however, for petrol rationing was introduced.

At the Brewery, P. A. Baker who had come as a pupil in 1939 was appointed Head Brewer. He had enlisted at the outbreak of war in the Nottinghamshire regiment, LAA. His war service took him to Alamein with the 8th Army and through all the way via Sicily into Italy, where he had the rare distinction of the immediate award, at the hands of General Alexander, of the Military Medal.

By 1957 the complete conversion of Fermenting Room No. 1 was finished and the decision made to start building Fermenting Room No. 3 in the area already cleared for this purpose. The capacity of Fermenting Room No. 1 was doubled from its original 1,200 brls. to its present capacity of 2,300 brls. No. 3 Room was deliberately planned to be built in two stages and was commenced in 1957.

Claude Chadburn, now seventy years of age, was glad to have the support and interest of his nephew, Robin, now thirty-seven, at the quarterly board meetings. It was forty-five years since Robin's father, eldest son of William Jackson Chadburn, had first joined the Brewery and thirty-five years since the death of Francis Chadburn.

In the year that Robin Chadburn was appointed a director Prime Minister Harold Macmillan was assuring the people that they had never had it so good; indeed, the affluent society, after the slight setback of the credit squeeze was becoming established. The habit of austerity, so long endured in England, was exploded by the swirling fashions of Christian

Dior. Men decided to break from austerity too, with brocaded waistcoats, narrow trousers, velvet collars. The cult of the Teddy Boy became a feature of British society.

The release from austerity brought a release of high spirits that was not always appreciated, particularly when it developed into violence that involved the community. Teddy Boys were involved in many unsavoury incidents, particularly unfortunate because they demonstrated that authority could be defied. There were race riots in nearby Nottingham.

The biggest talking point over the pints of the Mansfield Brew was the disaster to Manchester United football team in an air crash at Munich in 1958 when seven members of the party lost their lives.

1959 was the driest British summer for two hundred years and there were many splendid thirsts to be satisfied. At the height of the summer, however, the Brewery lost their trusted friend and adviser when S. C. Deakin died on 20th July 1959.

The National Coal Board announced that they proposed closing up to two hundred and forty mines in the next five years but the Mansfield area pits were to be the least affected.

The last British tram ran at Sheffield and, with it, the old order of life seemed to disappear. Supermarkets began to take the place of traditional trading, the number of cars on the roads doubled in the prosperous sixties, swamping towns and cities that fought back with restrictive parking and parking meters. The first Motorway had opened in 1959 between London and Birmingham.

The business of the Brewery proceeded under Claude's direction, with Jock Nangle and Robin Chadburn attending quarterly Board Meetings, and discussing between themselves the future of the Company, and in particular the two major holdings of Claude and Baily Thomas. In 1960 Nangle wrote to Claude expressing concern about future management and suggesting that a way should be sought to get Robin to give more of his time to the Brewery. It was realised that this might not be easy; he was living at Sudbrook between Grantham and Sleaford, farming there and heavily involved with Local Government, a J.P., Director of his father-in-law's Flour Mill in Lincoln and Vice Chairman of Central Wool Growers Ltd. – a sizeable farmers co-operative, besides the Architectural Practice with associated offices in Salisbury and Folkestone. Claude agreed that the approach be made and eventually Robin Chad-

A good contrast in No. 2 Fermenting Room between slate vessels and stainless steel, the latter increasing the capacity of that room and allowing space for the Yeast Propagation Plant.

burn became an Executive Director and Deputy Chairman, starting work on 1st April 1961. The same day that Dr. Beeching was appointed to his post in charge of British Rail's reorganisation.

At the same time Claude relinquished the Managing Directorship in favour of the joint appointment of J. B. Jenkins and Edward Deakin. Edward had clearly been very keen to have Robin join the Board as an executive, and had done all he could to educate him into believing that this was where his future should lie; another friendship had grown up over the previous three years that was to augur well for the Company. Jenkins administered the commercial side of affairs; was himself prominent in Local Government affairs, a J.P. like Claude, who interfered as little as possible in the way he ran his side of the business. Edward Deakin continued to produce the inimitable brew, to wield his considerable authority and to rule the production unit with a very firm hand from beneath the straw boater which was the very practical symbol of a Brewer in those days – acting as it did as a crash helmet among the pipes and fittings to be found in new positions every day as the Beer Mains are moved from one fermenting vessel to another.

There was a Census in Britain in this year and the population was shown to be 51,295,000.

On a sad note the Berlin Wall was built in this year. On a nostalgic note the Orient Express (Paris–Budapest), ran for the last time after seventy-eight years; and Bradshaw's *Railway Time Table* ceased publication.

Extensions to the productive capacity of the Brewery continued slowly. No. 3 Fermenting Room, which was planned to be built in two stages and which was commenced in 1957, was completed in its final form in 1962.

The Concert Room at the 'Oval', Sutton. The whole building cost £40,000 in 1961. The modernisation, 15 years later, cost the same sum.

13

Claude Chadburn was gratified to see his nephew, Robin, installed as an Executive Director of the Brewery. He thought back to the letter that Jock Nangle had written to him when he recommended Robin; in which he said that he had not suggested him because he was the Chairman's nephew and a Chadburn but because of his (Nangle's), assessment of Robin's all-round capacity to become the executive head of a big business.

Mr. J. T. Nangle's interest in Mansfield Brewery had commenced with his appointment as Trustee of the Baily Thomas Trust at the conclusion of the Second World War, and it was twelve years later that he had been appointed to the Board, and although he played no part in the day-to-day running of the Brewery he was there when needed as a top quality adviser. During the time between August 1957 and March 1961, when Nangle and Robin were non-executive Directors, they both gradually came to know each other and the peculiarities of the business, and few changes in the style of management were initiated. After all Pre-Tax Profits in 1926, after Claude took over, had been £72,000 and in 1961/62 were £500,000. Sales were increasing and modernisation of the plant was going ahead as fast as funds allowed.

In many family businesses, particularly breweries, the succession proceeds with the younger generation being trained by the older, thus becoming indoctrinated with established systems and habits, both good and bad. Robin Chadburn had an independent and successful career behind him when he came to the Brewery as a new boy. He was to be the proof that character and management ability mattered as much as technical experience and, in fact he believed this, and soon put it into practice in seeking another director, having found that the existing Board were approaching retirement age all together.

Claude was soon to be seventy-five, Munro-Thomas was never active. Jenkins, though only in the early sixties, was not able to carry on for very much longer. This would have left Edward Deakin and Robin as the only fully active Directors and the Brewer was naturally tied down on the technical side, being responsible for his own staff, for managing the Brewery itself, the Transport Department and the Bottling Department.

Robin, the new broom, could see that the management needed strengthening, that sales should be the responsibility of a Sales Director; he saw a great deal that needed attention at Director-level.

On his visits to Papplewick Hall he had met, and been much impressed by, David Weston.

David Weston was the tenant of Newstead Grange Farm on the Papplewick Estate when Robin first became a Director. He was clearly an outstanding farmer and personality. He was married to Claude's youngest daughter, Anne, and they lived at Newstead Grange where their four children, Julia, Johanna, Alan and Heather were born. Robin and David were very well known to one another and there was clearly respect in the relationship. In fact, before giving up his partnership in the Architectural Practice Robin had helped David and Anne to remodel the Grange and had brought oak window sashes from Hainton Hall to Newstead.

Soon after becoming an executive at the Brewery, with an eye to the future and a desire to continue a family involvement, Robin approached Claude, after discussing the possibility with Jock Nangle, to see if he would consent to an approach being made to David to sound out the possibility of his joining the Board, probably as Sales Director. After considering the prospects against his involvement with new agricultural engineering projects and ideas, David agreed and started to attend Directors' Management Meetings which, since Robin's appearance, were being held every fortnight.

Regrettably the considerable potential that David showed was never realised.

Anne and David frequently rode over from their farm to Papplewick Hall. Anne was an accomplished horsewoman, David less so. On one such occasion David rode over on his own to see his father-in-law. When the time came for him to leave Claude came out to say goodbye and then turned to go back through the impressive hallway.

A passing motorist on the roadway above was amazed to see a horse plunging and rearing in the forecourt of the big house, obviously endeavouring to unseat its rider who was leading a second horse. The motorist was even more amazed to see a man walking back into the house, quite deaf to the drama taking place behind him.

David Weston was flung from the horse on to the gravel drive. The motorist summoned an ambulance and alerted the bewildered Claude and the household. The ambulance came quickly but there was nothing they could do and David Weston never regained consciousness.

In 1963 Robin Chadburn was appointed Chairman of the Mansfield Brewery Company and Mr. Claude Chadburn, at the age of seventy-six, became the first President. It enabled him to spend more time at his beloved Papplewick Hall although he still took an active interest in the affairs of the Brewery and came in most days.

Mr. F. K. Munro-Thomas – the Captain – retired as a Director having been first appointed on the formation of the Limited Company thirty-eight years previously; this brought to an end the personal participation in Brewery affairs of the Baily interest.

Following the worst winter since 1881 there was some unemployment, and the figures rose at the beginning of 1963. But local unemployment had never seemed to have much effect on the Brewery profits – if anything in the short term there was more time to spend whiling the time away with a drink. Sales did drop slightly that year however and there was a break in an otherwise uninterrupted yearly increase in profits between 1935 and 1975.

Major modernisation schemes had been carried out at the 'Forest Tavern', Skegby, the 'Red Lion' at Farnsfield, the 'Stanton Arms' at New Houghton and the 'Wheatsheaf' at Bakewell.

Gambling was legalised in Britain and brewers were able to consider the desirability, or otherwise, of introducing 'one-arm bandits' into their premises. A gamble on a bigger scale occurred at Bridego Bridge, near Cheddington, where the Glasgow–London Mail was stopped by thirty men and robbed of two and a half million pounds, becoming known as the Great Train Robbery.

A more world-shattering crime occurred at Dallas, Texas

where President John Kennedy was assassinated. Unlike the dramatic accession to power of Lyndon Johnson our own leadership was involved in change and there were a number of hats in the ring following Mr. Macmillan's announcement from hospital that he would be giving up. Butler, Hailsham, Maudling and Heath were rejected in favour of Sir Alec Douglas Home.

The Beeching Report proposed closing half of the railway stations in the country and a third of the lines.

For Robin Chadburn the main preoccupation was the question of a replacement for David Weston.

In 1947 the daughter of the owner of the farm next door to Robin Chadburn had married Anthony Joseph Scruby. A qualified solicitor, he had specialised in commercial law and latterly had been Managing Director of a group of merchanting companies operating in East and Central Africa. In his younger days he had been a keen rugby player and turned out for the Lincolnshire County side. With previous Territorial Army experience, during the war he served with the Fourth Battalion, The Lincolnshire Regiment, which was in the same Brigade as the Eighth Battalion Sherwood Foresters. He left the Army as a Lieutenant Colonel. Whilst abroad he served for two years in Burma as a Brigade Major. Prior to, and during, the Mau Mau troubles he was a partner in a firm of solicitors in Nairobi, East Africa.

His family had previous connections with the brewing industry for his paternal grandfather was a wine importer and merchant in Saffron Walden, whilst the father of his maternal grandmother, Mr. W. B. Thorpe, was a maltster and brewer in Nottingham in the latter part of the last century.

On the day of David Weston's funeral Robin Chadburn telephoned Tony Scruby and told him what had occurred. It so happened that a week or so previously the two had been comparing notes at Sudbrook during one of the Scrubys' visits to Ann's parents, and both were consequently up-to-date with news of each other's affairs.

It says a good deal for Tony Scruby's adventurous spirit that he agreed there and then to talk over the possibility of coming to join Robin Chadburn and the company. Talks with Jock Nangle took place as early as August 1963, and within weeks his appointment to the Board was being confirmed.

Tony Scruby brought wide business and legal experience to

the Board of the company and within a few years, as Jenkins's health began to show signs of wear and tear, he was taking more and more responsibility for the administrative side of the Brewery's affairs. When Jenkins retired in October 1965 after 29 years, Tony Scruby took his position as Joint Managing Director with Edward Deakin, and this was the position for six years until September 1971 when Edward himself finally severed the Deakin connection that had lasted for fifty-three years and Tony Scruby took on the sole Managing Directorship.

Philip Baker followed Edward Deakin on to the Board in 1971 when his deputy, Michael Parsons, became Head Brewer. The Board then consisted of Robin Chadburn (Chairman), Tony Scruby (Managing Director) and Philip Baker as full-time executives with a vital role being played by Jock Nangle as an ever-ready guide and friend lending a very experienced hand to the whole of the company's policy. In fact it must be recorded that without Jock Nangle's help and the wisdom of his advice and influence, the future of the company as an independent entity might have proved almost impossible to preserve.

The discussions Robin Chadburn and Jock Nangle had with Claude about the company's future, and the preservation of Claude's fortune, led to Claude settling shares upon his daughters and their families, thus hopefully preserving the bulk of his share of the equity for the future. Robin became a Trustee, and in some respects was able to repay the careful stewardship of his own family's affairs by Claude in years gone by. There can be no doubt that when Claude retired, just before David Weston's death in June 1963, Robin's lot as succeeding Chairman was made very much easier by the remarkable trust that Claude immediately put in him.

Apart from Edward Deakin and, later, Philip Baker, direction of the company, was in the hands of Robin Chadburn, Tony Scruby and Jock Nangle, none of whom had been brought up in the brewing industry. Robin took up a place offered to him on the Council of the Brewers' Society and the contacts made there, together with the debates he could listen to, helped to make up a picture of the industry's traditions and approach to changing circumstances. In fact, later, he was appointed to the Executive Committee of the Society and became Chairman of one of the Sub-Committees.

Tony Scruby also took up a place later on the Law Committee and David Tyne (see frontispiece) on the Statistics Committee so, clearly, somebody thought that Mansfield Brewery had something to contribute, or was it perhaps that clashes over policy in the early days made the pundits feel that it was better to have people who might rock the boat readily to hand!

There had been clashes – perhaps emphasised by the particular trading area of the Mansfield Brewery, but brought about by Robin and Tony Scruby not always accepting the traditional approach (and nobody likes having his advice turned down).

One of the first approaches the two made was not to a brewer but to a petrol company, because it seemed that their business consisted of supplying liquids to tied outlets, and the running of their Estates had been subjected to scrutiny by the new Monopolies Commission who might one day get around to the brewing industry. Partly as a result of this it was decided to depart altogether from the accepted practice of collecting low rents on the public houses but charging the licensee more than the free trade for their beer. Clearly a pub between two clubs did not stand much chance of competing. The Tenancy Agreement was re-written and the tenants accepted the departure of 'Wet Renting' and the opportunity of making an additional profit on extra sales created by their own efforts. They did not like the high rents any more than the next man but it was fair, and the company began to put back into the upkeep of the properties the more realistic return on the capital involved, and Robin instituted a programme of maintenance procedures that resulted in a high standard in the licensed houses. At the time, the Brewers' Society was doing its best to avoid drawing attention to changes that it was obvious would have to be made one day, and questions in Parliament about Mansfield Brewery's rent increases did nothing to calm the situation down. In fact, visits to Mansfield from these very brewers, when the publicity died down, for advice on how to achieve the same end seemed to show that political necessity and practical commercial sense are not always easy to reconcile.

Robin Chadburn and Tony Scruby set about analysing the nature of the trade traditionally carried on by the Brewery in an attempt to assess carefully what was being achieved, and whether the service being given by the company was as good and as relevant to what was required as it could be, or whether fundamental changes should be considered. From previous re-

The 'Fairway', Sheffield. Jack Williamson, Managed House Director, is seen in the lower picture.

sults, and a rather more detailed look at the accounts that new methods of accounting and the installation of computers made possible, the fact that the company's fortunes depended upon the draught beer – the beautiful Mansfield Brew – became obvious.

The miners are cost-conscious, particularly experienced beer drinkers rather than spirit drinkers, and comparatively little wine other than fortified wines were in demand. A customer seemed to be either a 'club' man or a 'pub' man by habit, and whereas other breweries had sometimes fought a bit shy of the free trade of the miners' clubs, the Mansfield Brew had been sought by the customers themselves and, once installed, the Brewery had clearly been to great lengths to service those outlets to the very best of their ability. Edward Deakin and Philip Baker made it their business to see that deliveries were made as required and complaints dealt with personally and promptly.

The clubs, institutes and welfares were run by committees who were shown round the brewery at week-ends, when it was soon realised that the sooner you got round, the longer was the time available for a free drink at the end.

With the general rise in the standard of living these outlets started to look for ways of improving their own standards and this meant spending money. To some extent their popularity depended upon the cheap price – compared with the public house – at which they sold their beer, and there were not many committees who had been sufficiently businesslike or provident to accumulate funds with which to extend or refurbish. Discussions with the Brewery led to the company agreeing to lend money. The practice was gaining ground nationally and the proliferation of these outlets in the Midlands led to the demand being more common locally.

Generally the improvements meant an increase in trade, and prior to inflation the fund that the company could set aside for this purpose represented a sensible investment for both parties. Repayments were regular subject to the management ability of the committee concerned, and to start with the National Coal Board's Welfare Organisation very properly refused to become obligated to individual traders. Later, of course, when the Coal Board began to rely upon heavy subsidies from public funds this policy had to be reversed and these bastions of the working man's pint began to turn to the brewers for funds. The complication that this introduced was that their premises could not be offered as security, and up to that time the Brewery had been able to work on a very businesslike footing, only taking occasional risks by lending money to proprietorily owned clubs run for individual profit, and this practice was soon discouraged.

With the arrival of inflation the investment of money in loans quickly became very unattractive – by the time the money came back it was worth much less – and the cost of the necessary work escalated. This can perhaps be well illustrated by taking an example or two of building costs of new Public Houses over the period:

Completed		*Cost*
1963	'Rushley', Mansfield	£30,000
1967	'Cardinal', Sutton	£40,000
1971	'Pike and Heron', Tinsley	£50,000
1973	'Bell & Anchor', Scunthorpe	£60,000
1975	'Innings', Worksop	£150,000
1975	'Fairway', Sheffield	£180,000

Clearly in order to keep the shareholders' money properly employed meant finding a way of owning bricks and mortar rather than pound notes. Apart from the traditional public house, two methods were used. One was to emulate the club atmosphere and surroundings in tied outlets, retaining management control, and another was to build clubs and lease them to free trade organisations.

The first led to the establishment of the 'Aquarius' at Chesterfield, a very large 'Talk of the Town' type of entertainment theatre capable of serving over 1,000 meals in an evening, with continuous stage performances and the patrons seated at their own tables, booked in advance; a separate discotheque, and bars serving drinks up to 2 a.m. each morning. The lessons learnt from clubs who had been over-ambitious with the booking of star turns for stage performances had been well noted by Tony Scruby, and the scale of the operation, although a big risk for a small company, appears to have paid off under very experienced management. Something of the atmosphere of the old Music Hall was captured; something of the need for sophistication was catered for, particularly for young people who might otherwise have had to travel out of the Mansfield area for similar entertainment often at exorbitant prices. Of course fashions change – the 'Aquarius' was created out of a disused warehouse and set of offices – perhaps the time will come when by a complete rearrangement of the interior the function of the premises will need rethinking, and that was the spirit in which the investment was made.

Another such outlet, on a smaller scale, at Mexborough, did not come up to expectations because it would not hold sufficient people to justify the stage performances, but the very attractive interior has been the scene of television programmes and is hired out for functions.

The building of club premises for lease to other organisations at least enabled the Brewery to provide suitable accommodation for the precious beer and the other services necessary for bars and the provision of snack meals and so on. It is seldom realised that an architect is doing well to get the service area of a public house, including accommodation for the licensee, down to 60 per cent of the total building, leaving 40 per cent as drinking area for the public. Smaller houses are often hard put to make more than 25 per cent of the total space available for drinking. Several sets of club premises have been built and it is some comfort to know that with proper management the beer can be properly looked after and served. So often it is all too difficult to convince a Committee, or indeed their advisers, that a proper pint requires the back up of painstakingly careful thought being given to cellars, delivery areas, bottle stores, refrigeration, and thousands of pounds worth of cellar and bar equipment.

14

On 4th April 1964 the new President, Mr. Claude Chadburn, officiated at the opening of the 'Rushley Inn', Mansfield, and in addition, major modernisation schemes were carried out at the 'Albert Inn', Staveley, the 'Devonshire Arms', Sutton, the 'Gate Inn' and the 'Great Northern Hotel', both at Shirebrook and the 'Wellington Hotel' at New Whittington. Later in the year another new public house, the 'White Swan', was opened at Mansfield Woodhouse. A reminder that they existed in a mining community – if reminders were necessary – arose out of a report that mining subsidence was threatening the 'Glasshouse Inn' at Codnor which would have to be rebuilt as a result.

The sale of party-sized cans, recently introduced, was going very well and was in itself an indication that bottles were losing ground to draught beer, now a more stable product capable of being enjoyed at home. At the same time the influence of women was being felt more and more. It was this that was responsible in some measure for the refurbishing and carpeting of the clubs that increased the applications for financial help. In the pubs themselves, higher standards were being offered by the Brewers, and the wives of hardened club drinkers were demanding to be taken out to these larger than life home-from-homes with carpets in the cloakrooms. The old idea of a pub as man's exclusive domain in a tough spit-and-sawdust environment had gone.

Whatever the reasons for the popularity of the Mansfield Brew the sales of it continued to expand. So long as the quality remained constant it was clearly the drink that people wanted. In this connection the brewery giants, who were taking over smaller breweries on quite a large scale, were not endearing themselves to taken-over customers by replacing well-loved local brews with national brews. Because the Mansfield

The 'Spaniard', Wakefield

Brewery was able to resist change, and because the Mansfield Brew remained constant, the production of it was increasing at twice the national rate.

This caused a good deal of head scratching at Littleworth in the production department and the decision was taken to build and equip No. 4 Fermenting Room and also to complete the conversion of No. 2 Fermenting Room.

Despite an increase in Excise Duties in April of about 10 per cent on spirits, beer, wines and tobacco and a 15 per cent surcharge on wines and spirits in November the net profit for the year amounted to £661,152.

The installation of bulk beer facilities was engaging attention, and such progress had been made in the bulk handling of beer in perfect condition that it was now possible to deliver from the brewery to the public house by tanker. It meant, of course, the installation of tanks in those public houses suited by construction and trade to receive them. Once installed, the system guaranteed a perfect pint of beer every time and much less work for the cellar-man.

To characters known as hardened beer drinkers the very idea of delivering their beautiful brew in a tanker was almost bordering on the sacriligious; and yet the proof of the pudding soon proved to be in the drinking.

The now familiar company motif was introduced in 1964 and it made its debut in a new advertising campaign to spread the message of the Mansfield Brew wider still and wider.

The younger Brewery employees, like other youthful workers everywhere, were influenced by the many diversions of the affluent society; boring occupations like playing cricket or football had no hold upon them as it had on their fathers. The Brewery Sports Club, now little used, was wound up and the playing field was sold.

At this time Sir Alec Douglas Home departed from Downing Street to make way for Mr. Wilson who, in October 1964, was elected with a majority of 4.

In the year that Sir Winston Churchill died (at the age of ninety-one), the Brewery commemorated his life by naming a new pub after him, the 'Sir Winston' at Annesley Woodhouse. Another new public house opened was the 'Oval Inn' at Sutton-in-Ashfield and two public houses were purchased, the 'Lord Nelson' at Ambergate and the 'Vernon Arms' at Nottingham.

The extension of club popularity was linked with the modernisation and improvement of public houses. In increasing numbers the womenfolk were joining their men on an evening out and the delightful, old-established habit of standing at a bar knocking back pints of Mansfield Brew did not appeal to women. The trend towards entertainment, as opposed to straight drinking, was to continue, of course, even to the extent of Mansfield Brewery owning clubs of their own as we have seen. Meanwhile they took advantage of the recent relaxation in the gaming laws and decided to instal 'one-arm bandits' or gaming machines. Some there were who did not appreciate any diversion from the serious business of drinking and it was necessary to be selective in the siting of gaming machines. Music making machines or juke boxes had an equally mixed reception. Television was installed in many bars but lost more adherents than it gained; many had looked upon their pub as a refuge from the intrusion of the small screen. Television commercial advertising was dealt a blow at this time by the banning of cigarette advertising by Government decree.

The Government also announced a most unpopular measure, the Capital Gains Tax. The Opposition voted Mr. Edward Heath as Leader of the Conservative Party.

The two years that Robin Chadburn had as Deputy to Claude, before taking over the chair, had convinced both him and Jock Nangle that steps must be taken with regard to management procedures, particularly accountancy, regarding which there was nothing about the existing arrangements that escaped Nangle.

There was no organised Sales or Marketing structure; little control over capital expenditure related to cash flow forecasts; great freedom for architects regarding cost control on building work, no management accountancy, and little effective budgeting or monitoring of profit performance during the year. It was virtually left to the auditors to say what the profit had been each year, and these results had solemnly been reported at an Annual General Meeting held in the Boardroom, to very few shareholders. No Chairman's Statement had ever been circulated to shareholders with the accounts until that of Claude Chadburn when he retired in June 1963.

To start with, Management Consultants were brought in to establish procedures for the hotel accounts, where unexplained cash losses all too often followed the dismissal of an all too cheerful barman. The Consultant's man on the spot was Peter

The 'Aquarius', Chesterfield

Watson – later to join the company and strengthen the management team, until he left to understudy the Managing Director of the Burtonwood Brewery in Cheshire. Some 12 years later.

A second approach was made to the same Consultants regarding more general accountancy and office procedures, but it became clear that only the strengthening of the team within the Brewery itself would really result in the reorganisation that was necessary. It must be said once again that the way in which Claude, now President of the company, left Robin to tackle all these changes, without interfering or criticising, made it possible, with the help of Edward Deakin, the Company Secretary Fred Gleadell and, of course, Nangle. With Jenkins's retirement and Tony Scruby's appointment as Joint Managing Director the picture began to change because a management team below Board level was being built up capable of taking responsibility and, subject to being supplied with a proper backing from accounts and with the support of the brewing staff, these people were able to see that their contribution to the overall results was worthwhile; it justified the effort being put into management at all levels.

James Black Jenkins had joined the company in June 1935, when the pressures resulting from the purchase of the Chesterfield Brewery began to put a considerable strain on the administration. He became Company Secretary when Tommy Gilbert stepped down, and he became a Director, remaining Company Secretary, at the same time as Edward Deakin in 1946. In August 1956 when the two became Joint Managing Directors, Fred Gleadell took on the job of Company Secretary, and it was in September 1965 when ill-health forced Jenkins to give up the day-to-day anxieties of any Managing Director and retire. Jenkins had always played a prominent part in Mansfield's local government. Twice he had been Mayor, and when re-organisation resulted in a new District Council being established Alderman Jenkins, J.P., did not stand for re-election. During his time at the Brewery Jenkins's responsibilities had been considerable and it was not often that his recommendations were vetoed by Claude, who relied upon him and Edward Deakin to keep the internal wheels turning.

One of the first steps tackled by Tony Scruby was to provide help for Fred Gleadell, the Company Secretary, appointed in 1956 when Jenkins became Managing Director. As a qualified Accountant he had been responsible for the production of the

Annual Accounts in addition to being the Registrar, minuting the company's business, dealing with statutory notices, coping with legal contracts and all the other work of a professional Secretary to a public company. Fred Gleadell had joined the company in June 1950, and in 1976 has completed 20 years as Company Secretary. David Tyne joined the Brewery in 1965 and although he may have been surprised to find the simple and effective way in which business was done and reported, he was not the man to show any raised eyebrows, and he set about establishing procedures involving great changes, under Tony Scruby's appreciative direction. To ensure that this effort would be used to best advantage, steps were taken to divide and define responsibilities. In June 1964 Robin had already defined each Director's responsibility, and now it was the turn of Tony Scruby to pass this approach down the line throughout the main management functions.

The Brewery was left alone – its management and the resulting profit contribution were in Edward Deakin's more than capable hands, and to disturb Edward's style and lack of sympathy for accountants was clearly not a first priority. There are some troubles that even enthusiasts like Robin Chadburn and Tony Scruby can be excused for not courting. The whole process was clearly going to take some time so why start by disturbing the good?

The first priority had to concern marketing. Mansfield Brewery Sales Limited was created in 1965 following a complete revision of the company's credit control procedures. Revision is not perhaps quite the right word – a fairly friendly, haphazard approach had sufficed up to then, but the economic climate was such that greater efficiency was clearly required by all businesses if they were to survive, and that would apply to the tenant licensee and free trade clubs as much as anybody else. Any tightening of belts in that direction could soon squeeze the Brewery's bills off the top of the pile unless sanctions were applied, and from then on the supply of beer to non-paying customers was dramatically stopped. One or two outraged customers objected; a few left, to the relief of David Tyne who began to build up a much more businesslike relationship. Generally there was respect from customers and amazement from other breweries who were waiting in the wings in the hope of picking up a lot of new accounts.

The Sales Company operated by buying its products from

the Brewery and selling to retailers, be they tenant licensee, free trade or the Brewery's own managed hotels and public houses. The Directors – A. J. Scruby, J. D. Williamson and D. T. N. Tyne – were responsible for advertising, sales representation, promotions, customer relationships generally, and so on. Information monitoring performance was fed to them by David Tyne and it was up to them to deploy their efforts as best they might. Later, another subsidiary, to be known as Punch Bowl Entertainments Limited, to run the managed retail outlets, was set up and Jack (J.D.), Williamson took this new responsibility, handing over the marketing functions to Peter Watson who had been helping Robin Chadburn with the administration of the Tied Licensed Estate up to that time; coming as he did from a Management Consultancy background he had established well organised procedures in that department, and he took them with him as part of the new arrangement, and much later in 1975 Richard Umbers came to replace Peter Watson, when he departed to Cheshire. Both Richard Umbers's father and his grandfather had been Managing Director of the Barnsley Brewery. At last, in 1970, Management Accounts began to be produced for the Production and Delivery side of the Company's affairs and the cycle was complete. To the Central administration, now under Fred Gleadell and David Tyne, was added Hugh Wilson in 1973 when at last Tony Scruby was able to persuade his Chairman to give up the supervision of the company's Property Division. Robin Chadburn's experience of building and architects had clearly been more than useful to the company for many years. After all, most of the money made went into bricks and mortar, but his reluctance to give up the daily and increasing responsibility of checking on builders, contracts, purchases of land, architects etc., and liaising with other departmental heads was becoming an embarrassment, for arguing with the Chairman as one would like to argue with a colleague can be somewhat inhibiting. Hugh Wilson's father, a senior local government officer at Chesterfield, had been a good friend to the Brewery for very many years – sadly it was on his death that Hugh joined the company and had the job of implementing the major decision to convert over £1,000,000 of the Brewery's reserves of cash into Tied Outlets before inflation could do its worst with the falling value of those precious pound notes.

It says a lot for the company that in the one year, 1975, following the completion of the new cask filling plant, wine and spirit warehouse and beer tanker depot, and the provision of modern canteen and changing facilities, the company completed the building of six new public houses and the formation of modern offices out of the old wine and spirit warehouse, that at last brought everybody under one roof.

We need to go back however to 1966 to judge the background for these achievements in a proper light. In that year Harold Wilson was returned as Prime Minister with a majority of 97. The British economy was having one of its apparently inevitable sick spells and drastic medicine was being prescribed. There was also Selective Employment Tax and Corporation Tax to contend with. Somehow it was an unsettling time for British industry and there were extensive take-overs and mergers of companies.

Despite signs of a national malaise the Brewery maintained a most healthy condition with satisfactory increases in the sale of draught beers. Also, beer prices were increased to come in line with the already increased prices of competitors.

It was decided to allow draught Guinness to be sold in the Mansfield Brewery public houses. It was not a competitor with the Mansfield Brew in the sense that dedicated Guinness drinkers would not drink anything else; they would go where Guinness was available and might take potential Mansfield Brew customers with them. This was the first time the Brewery had ever sold anybody else's draught beer in its houses.

Another tidying-up financial measure was the sale of the premises of the old-established wine business of T. P. Wood, acquired with the Chesterfield Brewery.

The mining community were alerted and horrified by the Aberfan mining village disaster at this time. Continuous and torrential rain caused the landslide of a tip on to the village school of Aberfan resulting in the deaths of 116 children and 28 adults.

Under the Road Safety Act the police were authorised to give breath tests to car drivers and this had the immediate effect of limiting trade at those pubs which patrons could only conveniently reach by car. At first it was feared that police would be waiting to pounce outside pub car parks but after a week or so of apprehension it was found that this was not going to be so. Most regular drinkers realised perfectly well that quite a number of pub customers left at closing-time over the breathalyser limit but the admirable sense of British Fair Play was nevertheless outraged that police might apprehend them in car parks before they drove off. Responsible newspapers and the motoring organisations defended what they called the liberty of the individual.

The police stayed away from pub car parks and the trade crept back again.

Four new public houses were opened:- the 'Glass House Inn' at Codnor, the 'Eyre Arms' at Calver, the 'Three Lions' at Welbeck Colliery Village and the 'Cardinal' at Sutton Junction.

The 'Cardinal' was built in a circular shape resembling a cardinal's hat; it commemorates a visit by Cardinal Wolsey to a farmhouse in the vicinity.

Cardinal Wolsey, appointed Archbishop of York in 1514, was never formally installed in this office at York Minster. After some journeyings to and fro between his various palaces, such as Peterborough and Southwell, he started his journey to York in 1530 in preparation for his installation as Archbishop. At this time he was not in favour with Henry VIII, having spoken against the divorce of the King and Queen Katherine. The King ordered Wolsey's arrest for treason.

Having reached his palace at Scrooby (near present-day Bawtry), the King's Guard arrested him and he started his journey to London to stand trial. The route followed the ancient track, known as the Great Way, through Sherwood Forest which is thought to have run along what is now the Coxmoor Road which lies a quarter of a mile north-east of Sutton Junction. The Cardinal spent a night at the house of the Earl of Shrewsbury, whose mansion, Kirkby Hardwick, still exists and lies about three quarters of a mile to the south-west.

By this time the Cardinal was ill with dysentery and his journey ended prematurely at Leicester Abbey where he died before he could be called to account.

The old Meadow Foundry site opposite the Brewery in Littleworth, and adjoining the site of the old 'Ram Inn' with such historic Brewery connections, was purchased for future development.

The British economy was still under considerable pressure and the £ was devalued by 14.3 per cent.

Although many mines were threatened with closure the trade of the Mansfield Brewery was not affected. Sales of draught beer continued to increase and the new Bulk Beer Hall

A considerable contrast. Half the beer produced now leaves the Brewery in Bulk Tankers, all insulated and all cleaned and filled under cover and by automatically controlled processes. Eric Jackson, the Supervisor, is in touch personally with the customers who take beer from him.

was able to cope with the demand, due to considerable foresight when it was built.

The company's tenants went on an outing to York Races – partly to mark the firm's appreciation for their co-operation over the new Agreements now in force all round – and this is still talked of as having been a particularly cheerful occasion, with a good deal of discussion about changes like colour television and the breathalyser, the licensing of supermarkets and the likelihood of people being separated from the pint in the pub.

There was also talk of travel abroad which the British people had taken to in their millions during recent years; so much so, in fact, that Mansfield Sales Limited were tempted to go after a slice of this lucrative trade by setting up as Travel Agents in Belgium in an effort to lure the Continentals over here for a change. The balance of payments sorely needed more foreign currency to be earned and it was hoped that Government help, perhaps by way of tax relief, might be forthcoming. The traditional Mansfield Brew would never stand being exported, so why not try and entice foreigners over to drink it here.

The tanked beer, or bulk beer sales, increased through the subsidiary sales company specially set up for this purpose and based at Chesterfield. It was evident that this was the trend of future progress and as part acknowledgement of it 6-gallon casks were dispensed with.

As the tanked beer sales increased so the sale of spirits declined but this was probably not so much a result of the competition from 'perfect' beer as from the last imposition of duty on spirits. Whisky and gin drinkers had obviously changed their drinking habits since the last Budget, although not to wine despite an increase in wine sales, and certainly not to minerals which were also selling in bigger quantities; spirits drinkers are rarely satisfied with anything less potent and it is likely that they drank less or bought by the bottle at supermarket prices to drink at home.

Drinkers generally were tempted in increasing numbers to try their luck on the 'one-arm bandits' and the profits from the fruit machines helped in a small way towards the ever-increasing building costs.

New licensed premises acquired were the 'Green Dragon' at Oxton and the 'Willington House Hotel' near Repton. Major improvements and modernisation were carried out at the

'Queen's Hotel', Bakewell, the 'Duke of Wellington', Kirkby, the 'Gardener's Arms' at Chesterfield, the 'Crown' at Tibshelf, the 'Spread Eagle' at Chesterfield and the 'Bird-in-Hand' at Blidworth. Another off licence was sold, this time at Kirkby-in-Ashfield.

The Brewery has a long tradition of being fortunate in keeping a large proportion of those who work for it. The old family connections may well have something to do with this, the comparatively small numbers involved probably help, the Deakin management must have had considerable influence on the brewery side – certainly there is still a feeling of personal involvement, born perhaps of everybody knowing nearly everybody else. The people sitting at desks must often envy the lorry driver having what they imagine to be a carefree life outside, and perhaps the other way round as well – at least they both seem to realise that one cannot operate without the other. In 1970 it was decided that long service should be recognised and awards were made to 26 people.

	years of service
Alf Ansell	38
Ron Allen	38
Freddie Burton	30
Ernest Chamberlain	30
Arthur Chapman	49
Bob Gilliatt	44
Jim Halpin	45
Fred Hensleigh	33
Bill Holland	31
Percy Holmes	47
Doug Kemp	32
Mev Marriott	39
Ray Mellors	39
Les Pearson	37
Henry Peet	42
Ken Perry	32
Jack Revill	32
Percy Revill	44
Albert Rowley	50
Les Taylor	34
Sid Tyler	42

The 'Bench and Bar', Nottingham

Jim Wain	32
Graham Wilson	34
Les Yates	34

The President, Claude Chadburn, topped the lot with a record of 64 years service and Joint Managing Director Edward Deakin was well placed with 41 years. A person who could claim a long association with Mansfield Brewery, though hardly a working one, was Frank K. Munro-Thomas who died in 1970. He had retired as a Director in 1963, a position he had held, if somewhat formally, since the formation of the Limited Company in 1925. His death would have stirred in Claude Chadburn memories of his father's struggles to get hold of money, of his appeals to Gertrude and to Captain Thomas as he was then and to the implacable Verrall. The Lieutenant Thomas who had come into the life of the Mansfield Brewery during the First World War would trouble them no more.

A member of the Mansfield Brewery family who was more genuinely missed was Tom Hinchley who had joined the company in 1903, served in the First World War, and retired as General Foreman in 1963.

15

The active members of the Mansfield Brewery 'family' were called upon to renew their efforts as beer consumption increased, indeed the national consumption of beer reached record levels. The installation of a new copper helped with production.

In the East Midlands the drinkers went for their draught Mansfield Brew in preference to other drinks despite a first ever increase of 2d. a pint and the Brewery experienced a 4 per cent decline in the sale of bottled beers against the national trend.

History was made towards the end of 1969. Many a partaker of the Mansfield Brew will have wandered homewards on a crystal clear night under the light of a bold bright moon upon which, incredibly, a man was standing. It was the year when Neil Armstrong, Commander of U.S. Spacecraft 'Apollo II', became the first man to set foot upon the moon.

Despite the growing success of the Mansfield Brew there was one major problem that overshadowed all others. The Baily Thomas Trust owned half the Brewery; the person for whom the Trust had been created, Frank Baily Thomas, was not capable of making a will. On his death, therefore, the whole of his fortune would be taken by the Crown. There were no known relatives apart from his father, Captain Munro-Thomas who, as we have seen, was to die in 1970.

In 1969 Jock Nangle initiated a search, through the Salvation Army, in the forlorn hope of finding a long lost brother of the Captain who had emigrated to Canada. This brother, Hector, had not been heard of for fifty years and was presumed dead. The Salvation Army reported that Hector was alive and living within a short distance of Captain Munro-Thomas and his unfortunate son. All along the Captain had insisted that he must be dead, and neither had any particular desire to meet.

A change in the law at this time permitted the Court of Protection to approve the making of a Will – through the Receiver – by a person who lacked testamentary capacity but whose affairs were under the jurisdiction of the Court. In 1970 a Judge of the Chancery Division approved a Scheme whereby the greater part of Frank's fortune was divided between a Charitable Fund dedicated to research into mental illness, and a fund for the benefit of Brewery employees. In this way both Frank's disability and the source of his wealth were recognised. The Court, instructed by Mr. Nangle, seemed to recognise that they held in the balance the future of a successful company, and from that day it can fairly be said that everybody at the Brewery started to work as much for charity and themselves as for any other shareholder.

Mansfield Brewery sales created an all time record in 1970 and it was undoubtedly due to the increasing popularity of tanked beer which, for the first time, was giving a perfect pint at perfect temperature every time. Tanked beer sales forged ahead and sales of cask draught beer lagged behind. The productive capacity of the Brewery was now 6,500 barrels a week, a far cry from the original 500 barrels of Baily, Hage and Watson.

The Brewery opened a new pub, the 'Pike and Heron' at Tinsley on the outskirts of Sheffield. The 'Royal Hotel' at Mansfield Woodhouse and the 'Wagon and Coals' in Mansfield were sold.

Working men's clubs had always been popular in the north and they were spreading into the northern part of the Mansfield Brewery country. They flourished where there was a need for them and their presence may well have indicated a dividing line between the gregarious North and the reticent South. Clubs were also being improved and smartened up, provided with carpets and comfortable furnishings, aiming to cater for and to entertain the women and the family whilst providing the man with his pint. The clubs were still undercutting the pubs for price and they had other licensing advantages, besides being able to offer greater awards through their fruit machines.

At Whittington Moor the 'Queen's Hotel' had undergone improvements in recent months, reviving memories of the world famous names associated with it. Landlord Fred Davis moved to the 'Queens' in 1911 and his two sons, Joe (then aged ten), and Fred, were intrigued to find there a full-size billiard-table. Had there not been a billiard-table at the 'Queen's

Less men are required to roll barrels in these days of fork-lift trucks. The old 36 gallon standard wooden casks have given way to the 22 gallon, (100 litre), metal casks. The supervisors today are, (from left), Jack Revill, (Transport), 38 years service, Sid Tyler, 48 years, Jim Wain, (Transport), 38 years and Harold Moore, (Warehousing).

Hotel', Whittington Moor perhaps Joe Davis might not have become world billiards champion in 1926 nor, with his brother Fred, dominate world snooker from 1927 to the 1970s.

It was a year of news in the power industries. Electricity was in trouble with power cuts caused through industrial disputes, but the oil industry was favoured with discoveries of oil in the North Sea.

The major event of 1971 in the brewing history was the retirement of Edward Deakin. He had joined the Brewery in 1928 under his father who was the first qualified Head Brewer at Mansfield. Appointed a Director in 1946 he had succeeded to the position of Head Brewer on his father's retirement in 1947. Edward Deakin was appointed Joint Managing Director in 1956 and was then succeeded as Head Brewer by Philip Baker.

The Deakins, father and son, thus gave fifty-three years of service to the Mansfield Brewery (and to the brewing trade generally for Edward Deakin was a Past President of the Brewers' Guild). There is no question that the success of the Mansfield Brewery is a testimonial to their dedication and integrity. Their daily walk through the Brewery would be reminiscent of Captain's Rounds in a warship but the Deakins needed no bugler to warn of their coming. They were disciplinarians not for the sake of discipline but in the cause of perfection and, because of this, they were respected. They possessed the instinct, alas not often found in British management, to impose unquestioned discipline whilst at the same time inspiring a warm friendship.

If proof was needed of the success of the Deakin family in perfecting the Mansfield Brew it was provided by the sales figures for the year – a new sales record. The bulk bitter beer once again made the major contribution to sales but increased production was also needed of the beers in smaller containers.

Plans for rearranging and modernising brewery departments to achieve greater efficiency included the rehousing of the wines and spirits department, a new beer tanker service station and completely new accommodation for cask filling, all to go on the 35,000 square feet of land recently acquired from the Railways Board; land that William Jackson Chadburn had sold many years before. With the new cask filling plant the Brewery turned over to metal casks. It was a sad day for the strict traditionalists, and very much the end of an era. There were a great many wooden barrels (36 gallons) and hogsheads (54 gallons) that with expert cooperage had been in service for 40

The first four 250 barrel tanks for storing Marksman Lager. Insulated and chilled they stand on the roof of the Bulk Beer Hall. Fred Hemsley, (left), supervises the work in this building and has been with the Company 39 years. Alf Ansell, (44 years), looks after all cask filling.

years, and what wonderful containers they were. Each one handmade from seasoned oak with metal hoops, and each one a masterpiece of craftsmanship – remember that the ungrooved butted joints of each stave had to withstand a very great pressure from within when that much beer was shaken up on a lorry, and yet one skilful man could handle 5 cwt on his own, rolling and upending, and with the help of a mate setting rows of such casks up ready for tapping in due course. With one eye on the probable introduction one day of compulsory metrication, a very sizable investment in just two sizes of metal casks was made – 11 gallon (50 litres) and 22 gallon. They are obviously easier to handle but will never have the character, or to be fair, some of the drawbacks of the old wooden cask.

The 'Van Dyk Hotel' at Barlborough was bought. The 'Red Lion' at Birchover was sold, also three off licences at Mansfield Woodhouse, Newton and Ripley. The 'Lord Byron' and the 'Rifle Volunteer' were exchanged for the 'Crown and Cushion' and the 'Malin Wine Vaults' at Derby.

The bulk beer hall linked to the tanker delivery service was a success from the start. Sales again achieved new records and there seemed to be no end to the demand for the Mansfield Brew.

Success stimulates success. Far from accepting the new record sales with complacency the Board attacked the improvement of sales outlets with the gusto that Robin's grandfather had shown over seventy years before. The achievements of 1972 read like William Jackson Chadburn at his fifty-year-old best; and as a matter of interest the grandson was much the same age when construction was completed of the 'Aquarius' at Chesterfield and the 'Jesters' at Mexborough; also the 'Bell and Anchor' in the new shopping centre at Scunthorpe; the acquisition of the 'Keresforth Hall Hotel' at Barnsley and the deal to take in the 'Malin' and the 'Crown and Cushion' at Derby; as well as modernisation and enlargement at the 'Crown and Woolpack', Sutton, the 'Ladybrook' at Ling Forest, the 'Oak Tree' and the 'Rufford' in Mansfield, the 'Little John' at Ravenshead and the 'Spital' and 'Hollingwood Hotel' at Chesterfield. Sites were purchased at Balby, Rossington and Doncaster, and at Birley Wood golf course, Sheffield.

All this activity was achieved against the background of a miners' strike in the early part of the year, in fact it lasted from 10th January to 28th February 1972.

Bulk delivery of malt from East Anglia. Talking to the driver is Leslie Yates, Supervisor responsible for cellar conditions.

A modern sugar tanker delivering bulk liquid sugar to heated storage tanks; the Copperside Supervisor, Sid Clifford, is checking the dip.

At the outset of the strike the Brewery had coal supplies for fourteen weeks but it was soon apparent that shortage of electricity would be the main problem.

Beer stocks were increased marginally. After three weeks the Electricity Board was rationing the power supply and the Brewery took to brewing at night.

Even after the strike ended power cuts continued for a short while but the Brewery survived better than most, thanks to the willing cooperation of the employees.

The likely effect of V.A.T. was a problem, particularly in the administration of it at a time of staff difficulties and shortage.

In the Brewery the new cask filling hall, bulk beer dispatch and wine and spirit warehouse were proving their worth but the fuel crisis was causing anxiety regarding diesel supplies.

To take full advantage of the popularity of tanked beer sales which, of course, required suitable refrigerated storage tanks at the licensed premises, it was decided to refrigerate the draught beer cellars of all tied houses. The same freedom of decision obviously did not apply at the free trade outlets but everything was done to help them serve beer in perfect condition.

The cost of building the 'Sportsman' at Doncaster in 1974 almost equalled the whole capital of the Brewery in 1901. The sum needed to build the 'Fairway Inn' at Birley Wood was even greater. Decisions were taken to go ahead, however, and in addition the rebuilding of the 'Kings Head' in Mansfield was planned.

History is made by change, and industry can all too seldom afford to be nostalgic or indulge traditional methods in the face of the hard economic facts, and another blow to the company was the ill-health of the Malting Supervisor – Bob Gilliatt. It was his father before him – an impressively large and forceful character – who had years before during the General Strike in 1926 held the workforce steady when outsiders had tried to get them out on strike. His formidable figure astride the Brewery gates did as much to flatten the other side as his choice if direct turn of phrase! With his son's pending retirement it would not be worth initiating a new generation into the ancient mysteries of traditional floor malting in an un-air-conditioned building. Certainly up to that time a proportion of very high-quality malt had been coaxed out of the facilities offered, but often only due to the skill of the brewers and Bob, working against unfair odds. At about the same time, the future of bottling was at stake, and in that department Percy Holmes had held sway for many years with his school friend of fifty years previously – Sid Tyler. Percy's father had joined the Brewery in 1894 and Percy in 1922, ending yet another family tie, this one lasting 78 years. Bottling ceased in 1975, and in 1976 the manufacture of soft drinks at the Brewery also came to an end. The Tyler family make up yet another saga. Sid's father had joined the Brewery in 1903 as an experienced horseman, and had 'moved' Percy on a brewery wagon in 1922. He died in 1925, and his wife took on the job of office cleaner, becoming a trusted employee for 20 years. Young Sid started in 1927 and with the 12 years worked by his brother will complete an aggregate of 100 years with the company.

Ever since February 1966, when the replacement of the old slate fermenting vessels with stainless steel and the second (No. 4), new Fermenting Room was completed, expansion plans for the Brewery had been constantly in hand and during the whole of that time the production of the company's own lager was shelved because the capacity of the Brewing staff to cope with new equipment was being constantly overtaxed. Traditional brewing methods were still jealously preserved and traditional materials used, with all the seasonal problems of harvest and growing conditions, and the Board made it difficult for the brewers to keep their heads above that of the beer.

It was recognised that essential priorites to maintain the quality of the traditional brew must come before the introduction of a new product. Planning for lager went ahead, however, but it was not until April 1975 that final authority to purchase equipment could reasonably be fitted into the Capital Programme and added to the workload; by then extensive test marketing was approved and careful development of new brewing techniques completed. The name 'Marksman' was settled upon for the new lager, as was the method of dispensing and the design of the equipment to ensure that the customer would be happy with this latest addition to the draught Mansfield Brew.

The era of William Jackson Chadburn was a story of adventuring; the era of Claude Chadburn was one of consolidation. They were both central to the style they created, they were seen to be playing their part.

In the twelve years of Robin Chadburn's Chairmanship there has been greater real progress than in the previous hundred years. The solution of the Baily Thomas Trust prob-

The stone wall on the right of these views identifies the photographer's stand. The Brew House, built in 1906, has remained the heart of the Brewery; extensions have been grafted to this central block. The new office entrance – by the parked cars – seems to dominate the Brewery but in fact this is dwarfed by the extensions now operating.

Hops are still collected from cold store on the Brewery's own vehicles and the lower picture shows one of a fleet of 18 modern lorries that are principally used for the delivery of cask and bottled beers.

lem was thought up by Nangle in his time – and without such a solution the Mansfield Brewery might well have been engulfed by a take-over on the death of the last of the Baily line. Under his leadership the Brewery has not been inhibited by tradition; in addition to introducing tanked beer a new management structure has been created and a wide new range of benefits brought in; it looks now as though the company has another winner in the new Mansfield Marksman Lager.

What, one wonders, would William Jackson Chadburn have thought to see it all . . . the automated brewing systems, the computers, the tanked beer? We can be quite certain that he would not only have approved but he would have been exceedingly proud.

A BRIEF OUTLINE OF THE BREWING PROCESS

RAW MATERIALS

The essentials of brewing have changed little over the centuries. The ingredients of beer are still malt (made from barley), hops, sugar, yeast and water. Hops provide aroma, flavour, bitterness and preservative qualities, sugar contributes to the colour and flavour of the final product, and malt provides most of the fermentable material. Yeast converts sugar and malt extract to alcohol in order to obtain energy for its life processes. The yeast employed is a single pure strain, peculiar to this brewery, and is periodically propagated to ensure purity.

1. *MALTING*

BARLEY ↓	Starch filled grain (with a husk)
STEEPED ↓	Soaked in water for approximately 48 hours to absorb sufficient moisture to grow.
GERMINATION ↓	7 days controlled growth during which time rootlets and a shoot appear. Biochemical changes take place, which are basically the production of enzymes which are capable of converting starch to sugar.
KILNING ↓	Careful drying of the barley after growth to arrest the changes taking place but without inactivating the enzymes. The temperature of kilning affects the colour of the malt and hence that of the final beer.
STORAGE	The malt (physically similar, but different internally to barley) can now be stored in a dry state until required.

Briefly, the principle of malting is to modify the barley to a state where the starch can be, and has begun to be, converted to sugar. No further action takes place after drying so the malt is held in a 'dormant' state until mashing.

The brewery no longer performs its own malting but buys its malt under rigid specification from maltsters outside the company.

2. *BREWING*

MALT ↓	Usually delivered in bulk and stored in grain hoppers.
SCREENING ↓	Removal of rootlets and extraneous matter by sieving.
MILLING ↓	Cracking and grinding of the malt to a coarse flour keeping the husk reasonably intact. The resultant material is commonly called 'grist'.
MASHING ↓	Mixing of the grist with hot water at a selected and carefully controlled temperature (145–155°F), in a mash tun. The mash is left to stand for one hour for the enzymes (now reactivated) to complete the conversion of starch to sugar.
SPARGING ↓	The fermentable sugars are extracted from the malt by continually spraying hot (170°F) water on top of the mash as the extract is drawn off at the bottom of the mash tun. This continues until all the required sugar has been extracted. Spent grain is discharged from the mash tun and sold as an ingredient of cattle feed.
WORT ↓	The extract obtained from the malt in the mash, comprises mainly of sugar, proteins and amino acids, and is called 'sweet wort'.
BOILING + HOPS & SUGAR ↓	The sweet wort is collected in a copper and boiled for about $1\frac{1}{2}$ hours in the presence of hops. During boiling, enzymic activity is destroyed, the bitterness is extracted from the hops, the wort is sterilized, and a solution of undesirable substances, mainly denatured proteins, is precipitated. Sugar is also added at this stage to enhance the flavour of the final beer.
HOP BACK ↓	The boiling wort is cast into the hop back where the spent hops are separated. Spent hops may be used commercially as a fertilizer.
COOLING ↓	The wort is cooled to about 63°F before being run into Fermenting Vessels.
FERMENTATION	As the wort is collected in the Fermenting Vessels yeast is added. The quantity and gravity of the beer in each vessel is then declared to the Customs and Excise. Over the next 3 or 4 days the temperature is allowed to rise to about 70°F and the yeast breaks down sugar to alcohol and carbon dioxide. Carbon dioxide is collected and used to carbonate the beer at a later stage. Other side reactions occur in the Fermenting Vessel contributing to the

flavour of the product. The yeast also multiplies and is re-used. The excess yeast is sold (a yield of about 6 times the original yeast used is normally obtained), and is used in such products as "Marmite", "Yeast Vite" etc.

3. *PROCESSING*

BEER IN F.V.	Beer remains in the Fermenting Vessel for 7 days after which time fermentation is complete and cooling has begun.
↓ PRIMINGS & FININGS	The beer is then pumped to the receiving cellars. Primings (sugar) and Finings (Isinglass) are added en route.
↓ RECEIVING CELLAR	The beer is kept at about 60°F for 2 or 3 days to allow the fining action to take place i.e. the yeast and protein precipitates out.
↓ CHILLING	The beer is chilled to 30°F to assist filtration. The beer is now carbonated to varying degrees, depending on the way it is to be packaged, with the carbon dioxide collected from the Fermenting Vessels and cooled to 31°F using a plate heat exchanger.
↓ COLD BEER STORE	It is usually retained at this temperature for 2 or 3 days to complete yeast and protein precipitation.
↓ FILTERING	The yeast and protein are removed by filtration.
↓ COLD BEER STORE	The bright beer is collected in cold storage tanks until required.

4. *MARKSMAN LAGER*

RAW MATERIALS	The very best quality lager malt and German Hallertau high aroma hops are used for the brewing of 'Marksman' lager.
↓ FERMENTATION	The low temperature fermentation is carried out in very tall (450 barrel: 130,000 pints) conical fermenting vessels which aids natural carbonation and selectively encourages a very clean and sharp palate.
↓ LAGERING	After 7 days' fermentation the lager is carbonated and chilled to 31°F and held at this temperature for several weeks in a battery of tall 450 barrel cold conditioning tanks on the roof of the Bulk Beer processing department.
↓ FILTRATION	The lager is filtered in much the same way as beer.

5. *DISTRIBUTION AND PACKAGING*

After a rigid and complex routine of cleaning, the Bulk Road Tanks are filled with Mansfield Bitter and Mansfield Mild for delivery to our Public Houses and Free Trade Clubs.
All beer sales are carefully monitored by bulk flowmeters to ensure our customers receive the correct quantity of our high quality products.

CASK BEER

After a very rigorous cleaning process, during which the casks are subjected to high temperatures with steam, the casks are filled with Mansfield Bitter or Mild Beer or 'Marksman' Lager. The casks are automatically filled by meter to ensure again that the customer receives the correct quantity in each cask and are subsequently check weighed.

CANNED BEER

Mansfield's Festive Fours are filled with the same high quality Bitter Beer specially prepared to achieve a longer shelf life in the fully seamed 4 pint cans which are individually check weighed to ensure each can contains the correct volume.

	Aquired or built*	Cost	Improved
DERBYSHIRE			
Alfreton			
Miners Arms	1899	£2440	1958
Ambergate			
Lord Nelson	1966		1970
Ashover			
Red Lion	1911 ex Chesterfield		1970
Bakewell			
Queens Arms	1921 ex Chesterfield		1969
Wheatsheaf Hotel	1921 ex Chesterfield		Rebuilt 1963 incorporating Anchor Inn
Barlow			
Peacock Hotel	1920 ex Chesterfield		1967
Baslow			
Robin Hood	1921 ex Chesterfield		Rebuilt 1960
Rutland Arms	1921 ex Chesterfield		1967
Wheatsheaf Hotel	1921 ex Chesterfield		1948 & 1968
Birley Wood			
Fairways	1975*		
Blackwell			
Blackwell Hotel	1898 ex Chesterfield	£600	1966
Robin Hood	1921 ex Chesterfield		1959
Bolsover			
Black Bull	1884 ex Chesterfield	£1210	1969
Blue Bell	1876 ex Chesterfield	£1100	1970
Carr Vale	1902 ex Chesterfield		1968 & 1975
Castle Arms	1959*		
Cavendish Hotel	1911 ex Chesterfield		
Brampton			
Anchor Inn	1890 ex Chesterfield	£1200	1921
Royal Oak	1920 ex Chesterfield		1960
Brimington			
Miners Arms	1874 ex Chesterfield	£400	

	Acquired or built*	Cost	Improved
Red Lion	1876 ex Chesterfield	£1480	1975
Three Horse Shoes	1886 ex Chesterfield	£2825	1938
Calow			
White Hart	1897 ex Chesterfield	£1840	1958 & 1975
Calver			
Derwentwater Arms	1920 ex Chesterfield		1961
Eyre Arms	1926 ex Chesterfield		Rebuilt 1967
Chesterfield			
Aquarius	1972		Created from Warehouse
Blue Bell	1886 ex Chesterfield	£1604	Rebuilt 1927
Bridge Inn	1902 ex Chesterfield		1968
Chesterfield Arms	1872 ex Chesterfield	£2100	1966
Gardeners Arms	1861 ex Chesterfield	£450	1969
Punch Bowl	1924 ex Chesterfield		
St. Helens	1881 ex Chesterfield	£1500	1973
Spital Hotel	1922* ex Chesterfield		1974
Spread Eagle	1888 ex Chesterfield	£4200	1969
Station Hotel	1892 ex Chesterfield	£9165	1962, 1963, 1974, 1975 & 1976
Clay Cross			
Elm Tree	1944 ex Hollis Trust		1963
Furnace Inn	1874 ex Chesterfield	£850	1966
Nags Head	1944 ex Hollis Trust		
Clowne			
Angel Inn	1888	£1693	Rebuilt 1961
Van Dyk Hotel	1972		1974
Codnor			
Glasshouse Inn	1883 ex Chesterfield	£950	Rebuilt 1968
Cutthorpe			
Cutthorpe Hotel	1929 ex Chesterfield		1976
Danesmoor			
Park House	1908 ex Chesterfield		1975
Derby			
Crown & Cushion	1972 ex Bass		1972
The Malin	1972 ex Bass		1973 & 1975

Duckmanton				
Duckmanton Hotel	1926	ex Chesterfield		
Eckington				
Royal Hotel	1923	ex Chesterfield		1966
Grassmoor				
Boot & Shoe	1897	ex Chesterfield	£4200	1954
Miners Arms	1944	ex Hollis Trust		1962
Heath				
Elm Tree	1954			1956 & 1966
Hollingwood				
Hollingwood Hotel	1926	ex Chesterfield		1972
Langwith				
Devonshire Arms	1956			
Gate Inn	1900			1974
Marsh Lane				
Fox & Hounds	1919	ex Chesterfield		1968
Milltown				
Miners Arms	1936			1966
Morton				
Live & Let Live	1946			1956
Newbold				
Dunstan Inn	1961*			1974
Nags Head	1928	ex Chesterfield		1959
New Houghton				
Stanton Arms	1899	ex Chesterfield	£4500	1963
Newton				
George & Dragon	1950			1961
New Tupton				
New Inn	1861	ex Chesterfield	£605	1970
New Whittington				
Crown Inn	1876	ex Chesterfield	£1800	1952
Miners Arms	1938			1964
Wellington Hotel	1859	ex Chesterfield	£900	1964 & 1975
North Wingfield				
Alma Inn	1944	ex Hollis Trust		1956 & 1975

	Acquired or built*		Cost	Improved
Spinning Wheel	1928	ex Chesterfield		1956
White Hart	1921	ex Chesterfield		1963
Old Whittington				
Cock & Magpie	1884	ex Chesterfield	£1050	1962
Pentrich				
Devonshire Arms	1967			1969
Pilsley				
Willow Tree	1944	ex Hollis Trust		1968
Pinxton				
Greyhound Inn	1886		£1529	1960
Miners Arms	1900			1959
Ripley				
Prince of Wales	1898	ex Chesterfield	£3200	1966
Railway Inn	1883	ex Chesterfield	£1000	1959
Thorntree Hotel	1876	ex Chesterfield	£2000	1965
White Lion	1891	ex Chesterfield	£3550	1961
Rowsley				
Grouse & Claret	1921	ex Chesterfield		1966 ex Station Hotel renamed after improvements
Scarcliffe				
Elm Tree	1880		£1070	1966
Shirebrook				
Gate Hotel	1900	ex Chesterfield		1964
Great Northern	1882		£1250	1966
Shirland				
Red Lion	1926	ex Chesterfield		1968
Somercotes				
Cotes Park	1962*			
Spitewinter				
Three Horse Shoes	1957			1961
Staveley				
Elm Tree	1897	ex Chesterfield	£6700	1967
Nags Head	1871	ex Chesterfield	£1250	1956
Railway Inn	1926	ex Chesterfield		1963
Stretton				
White Bear	1901	ex Chesterfield		1954

Swanwick			
Boot & Slipper	1892	£1045	1958
Tibshelf			
Crown Hotel	1871 ex Chesterfield	£2000	1969
White Hart	1882 ex Chesterfield	£700	1956 & 1962
Troway			
Gate Inn	1919 ex Chesterfield		1954
Tupton			
Woodthorpe Inn	1959*		
Whittington Moor			
Queens Hotel	1886 ex Chesterfield	£1500	1969
Whitwell			
Holmefield Arms	1955 ex Hornbys		Rebuilt 1960 renamed from "The Vaults"
Willington			
Willington House	1969		1970
Woodthorpe			
Albert Inn	1928 ex Chesterfield		1965
NOTTINGHAMSHIRE			
Annesley Woodhouse			
Forest Tavern	1886	£1127	1975
Sir Winston	1966*		
Blidworth			
Bird in Hand	1892	£1113	1969
White Lion	1898	£1287	1950 & 1958
Edwinstowe			
Dukeries Hotel	1895	(Site £560)	1969
Robin Hood	1955 ex Hornbys		Rebuilt 1957
Farnsfield			
Plough Inn	1955 ex Hornbys		1975
Red Lion	1883	£945	1964
White Post	1921 ex Chesterfield		1956, 1960 & 1966
Gunthorpe			
Unicorn Hotel	1937		1975
Huthwaite			
Peacock Hotel	1886	£1395	
White Hart	1893	£2125	1938

	Acquired or built*	Cost	Improved
Kirkby-in-Ashfield			
Duke of Wellington	1895	£3046	1969 & 1975
Railway Inn	1891	£3254	1969 & 1974
Mansfield			
Black Bull	1901 (Bull Hotel)		Rebuilt 1925 improved 1967
Bowl in Hand	1898	£3877	1964
Bridge Tavern	1896	£2866	1955
Brown Cow	1892	£1667	1966
Dial Hotel	1887	£3055	1965
Eclipse Inn	1885	£3379	Rebuilt 1962
Eight Bells	1895	£2910	Rebuilt 1925 improved 1975
Kings Arms	1875	£700	1975
Kings Head	1898	£2169	Rebuilt 1975
Ladybrook	1958*		1973
Ling Forest	1954*		1973
Market Hotel	1901		
Midland Arms	1900		1967
New England	1963*		
New Inn	1897	£4168	
Oak Tree	1934*		1973
Pheasant Inn	1879	£1100	1971
Portland Arms	1895	£3784	1975
Queens Head	1887	£2422	Rebuilt 1959
Railway Inn	1867	£800	1967 & 1975
Ram Inn	1961*		The Old Ram purchased 1926 moved to new site 1961
Ravensdale	1955 ex Hornbys		1975
Reindeer	1879	£2100	1967 & 1975
Rushley	1964*		1968 & 1975
Sir John Cockle	1937*		1959
Stag & Pheasant	1887	£2221	1960
Swan Hotel	1929		1960, 1967 & 1970
Victoria Hotel	1878 (White Bear)	£1100	Rebuilt 1925 improved 1965
Westfield Hotel	1895	£1967	1965
Wheatsheaf Hotel	1877	£1450	1954

William IV	1892	£2246	1969 & 1975
Ye Olde Ramme	1877	£1800	1974
Yew Tree	1889	£984	1960
Mansfield Woodhouse			
Anvil Inn	1884	£1081	1970 & 1974
New Inn	1888	£1400	
Parliament Oak	1880	£800	1937
Sunnydale	1956*		1975
White Swan	1880	£780	Rebuilt 1965
Meden Vale			
Three Lions	1968*		
Nottingham			
Bench & Bar	1975*		
Vernon Arms	1966		1971
Ollerton			
Ollerton House	1957*		1963 licence transferred from Royal Oak
Plough Inn	1889	£821	Rebuilt 1925 improved 1963
Oxton			
Green Dragon	1968		1973
Pleasley			
White Swan	1921		1938
Rainworth			
Robin Hood	1896	£3294	1967
Ravenshead			
Little John	1903		1961, 1968 & 1973
Selston			
Railway Inn	1887	£2501	1966
Skegby			
Forest Tavern	1887	£885	1963 & 1975
Southwell			
Crown Hotel	1955 ex Hornbys		1974
Sutton-in-Ashfield			
Apollo Tavern	1893	£2290	1966
Cardinal	1967*		
Cart & Horse	1883	£2000	1972
Crown & Woolpack	1893	£3352	1973

	Acquired or built*	Cost	Improved
Devonshire Arms	1894	£3300	1965
Mapplewells	1880	£700	Rebuilt 1963 improved 1974
Old Blue Bell	1880	£1370	1968
Oval	1961*		1975
Speed the Plough	1886	£1271	
Travellers Rest	1891	£1327	1956
SOUTH HUMBERSIDE			
Scunthorpe			
Bell & Anchor	1973*		
SOUTH YORKSHIRE			
Barnsley			
Keresforth Hall	1973		1974
Doncaster			
Alverley	1975*		
Grove Inn	1975		1976
Sportsman	1974*		Created from Golf Club premises
Rotherham			
Charter Arms	1976*		
Windmill	1970		1974
Sheffield			
Ozzie Owl	1971		1972
Tinsley			
Pike & Heron	1972*		
Worsbrough			
Cutting Edge	1976 ex Scottish & Newcastle		
WEST YORKSHIRE			
Wakefield			
Spamard	1976*		